# The Private Sector in State Service Delivery

Joan W. Allen
Keon S. Chi
Kevin M. Devlin
Mark Fall
Harry P. Hatry
Wayne Masterman

# The Private Sector in State Service Delivery: Examples of Innovative Practices

THE COUNCIL OF STATE GOVERNMENTS

THE URBAN INSTITUTE PRESS
Washington, D.C.

**THE URBAN INSTITUTE PRESS**
2100 M Street, N.W.
Washington, D.C. 20037

*Library of Congress Cataloging in Publication Data*

The Private Sector in State Service Delivery: Examples of Innovative Practices / Joan W. Allen, . . . [et al.].

Bibliography
1. Public contracts—United States—States.   2. Contracting out—United States—States.
HD3861.U6P75 1989      353.9'3711—dc19      89-30387 CIP

ISBN 0–87766–460–9 (alk. paper)
ISBN 0–87766–461–7 (alk. paper, casebound)

All Urban Institute books are produced on acid-free paper.

Printed in the United States of America.

9 8 7 6 5 4 3 2 1

Distributed in the United States and Canada by
University Press of America
4720 Boston Way                     3 Henrietta Street
Lanham, MD 20706                  London WC2E 8LU, England

SE . R

**THE URBAN INSTITUTE** is a nonprofit policy research and educational organization established in Washington, D.C. in 1968. Its staff investigates the social and economic problems confronting the nation and government policies and programs designed to alleviate such problems. The Institute disseminates significant findings of its research through the publications program of its Press. The Institute has two goals for work in each of its research areas: to help shape thinking about societal problems and efforts to solve them, and to improve government decisions and performance by providing better information and analytic tools.

Through work that ranges from broad conceptual studies to administrative and technical assistance. Institute researchers contribute to the stock of knowledge available to public officials and private individuals and groups concerned with formulating and implementing more efficient and effective government policy.

Conclusions or opinions expressed in Institute publications are those of the authors and do not necessarily reflect the views of other staff members, officers or trustees of the Institute, advisory groups, or any organizations that provide financial support to the Institute.

# ACKNOWLEDGMENTS

This book is the result of a joint effort by The Urban Institute and The Council of State Governments. Harry P. Hatry of the Institute was the overall project manager and one of the Institute authors. Other Institute authors were Joan W. Allen and Mark Fall. Douglas R. Roederer was the project leader for The Council of State Governments. The Council authors were Keon S. Chi, Kevin M. Devlin, and Wayne Masterman.

Valerie Nelkin of Bear Enterprises edited the volume. Kenneth P. Voytek of the State of Michigan provided materials for the study and assisted in the overall review process.

We are grateful to the Ford Foundation and Aetna Life & Casualty Foundation for providing funds for this work and to the states of Delaware and Maryland, which helped stimulate this work through earlier projects involving them, The Council of State Governments, and The Urban Institute.

# CONTENTS

**Exhibits**

# Chapter One

# INTRODUCTION

Harry P. Hatry

State agency managers are always under pressure to cut costs while ensuring the continuing quality of their services to the public. Theirs is a tough assignment! This book has three purposes:

1. To encourage state officials to consider innovative ways to deliver their services better and more efficiently, especially options that make more use of the private sector (whether private citizens, for-profit businesses, or nonprofit organizations);
2. To alert state officials to the problems encountered in undertaking such innovations; and
3. To encourage state agencies to undertake careful periodic examination of their programs, both to identify innovative options and to analyze them adequately to provide a realistic picture of likely costs, benefits, and pitfalls of both the options and the status quo.

To accomplish these purposes, we present examples of state agencies' using contracting, volunteers, vouchers, and public-private partnerships to help deliver services. We also identify problems encountered and, when available, give evidence of how successful these alternative ways of delivering state services have been.

A major impediment to the greater use of the private sector to deliver state services is the lack of knowledge about, and experience with, alternative approaches. This book is designed to help fill the gap.

## BACKGROUND

The use of the private sector to deliver public services has exploded since 1978, when California voters passed Proposition 13, a major fiscal containment effort. Proposition 13 was followed by numerous other state and local actions to contain costs. Such actions have continued. The election of President Reagan in 1980 brought in an administration that pressed hard for increased use of the private sector in delivering public services at all levels of government.[1]

Whatever the outcomes of future national elections, fiscal pressure on government budgets at all levels seems likely to continue for many years. In any case, seeking innovative service delivery approaches that can contain costs and improve the quality of state services is simply good public policy.

Greater use of the private sector is one potential way to contain costs and improve services. Of the three levels of government, the states have been the slowest to move in this direction as an explicit management strategy. Since passage of Proposition 13, many local governments have considered—and a considerable number introduced—greater use of the private sector, particularly through contracting for many services. The federal government has pressed hard to encourage state and local governments, but its own initiatives have not proceeded far. However, it has rejuvenated its "A-76" procedure, which requires explicit examination of federal commercial activities in terms of contracting for services. The federal government has also played a major role in encouraging use of the private sector for many services for which it has provided funds to state and local governments, transportation, health and social services, for example.

Approaches to use of the private sector vary from contracting to voluntarism. Exhibit 1.1 provides a list of such approaches. State governments, though as a whole quite familiar with these arrangements, have tended to limit their use to the more traditional "tried and true." Contracting, until recent years, has been limited primarily to construction of buildings and roads and other highly specialized services.

Increased use of the private sector has some major potential advantages as well as problems. Below, we first discuss some reasons for increased use of the private sector, identify some of the potential advantages, and then identify potential problems with private sector use.

## REASONS FOR GREATER USE OF THE PRIVATE SECTOR

Governments consider using the private sector to help deliver services for six basic reasons:

Exhibit 1.1  DEFINITIONS OF ALTERNATIVE SERVICE DELIVERY APPROACHES

1. *Contracting for service.* The government contracts with private firms (profit or nonprofit) to provide goods or deliver services. The government may contract to have all or a portion of a service provided by the private firm.

2. *Franchises.* The government awards either an exclusive or nonexclusive franchise to private firms to provide a service within a certain geographical area. Under a franchise agreement, the user pays the firm directly.

3. *Grants/subsidies.* The government makes a financial or in-kind contribution to a private organization or individuals to encourage them to provide a service so that the government does not have to provide it.

4. *Vouchers.* The government provides vouchers to clients needing the service. The clients are then free to choose the organization from which to buy the goods or services. Clients give the voucher to the organization, which obtains reimbursement from the government.

5. *Volunteers.* Individuals in the jurisdictions provide free help to a government agency. This approach, as defined here, is limited to volunteers who work directly for a government. It does not include individuals doing volunteer work for a private (for example, charitable) agency.

6. *Self-help.* The government encourages individuals or groups, such as neighborhood or community associations, to undertake for their own benefit activities that the government would otherwise have to undertake.

7. *Use of regulatory and taxing authority.* The government uses its regulatory (deregulatory) or taxing authority to encourage private sector organizations or individuals to provide a service or at least to reduce the need for public services.

8. *User fees and charges to adjust demand.* Users of a service are charged a fee based on how much they use the government-supplied activity, thus putting the fiscal burden on users of the activity. For the purposes here, we are not concerned with the use of fees and charges for the sake of raising revenues.

9. *Encouraging private organizations to take over an activity ("divestiture").* Here the government gives up responsibility for an activity but works with a private agency (profit or nonprofit) willing to take over responsibility. (This arrangement might involve a one-time grant or subsidy.)

10. *Demarketing/reducing demand for service.* The government attempts to reduce the need and demand for a government service through a variety of marketing techniques.

11. *Obtaining temporary help from private firms.* Private firms lend personnel, facilities, and equipment or even provide funds to the government.

12. *Joint public-private ventures.* Businesses and the government join forces for ventures such as a major new economic development or revitalization project.

Source: Adapted from Harry P. Hatry, *A Review of Private Approaches to the Delivery of Public Services* (Washington, D.C.: Urban Institute Press, 1983).

1. *To obtain special skills or supplement staff for short periods.* Contracts for such professional services as those of architects, engineers, auditors, and consultants are in this category. States have used private organizations and private individuals (consultants) for this reason for many years.
2. *To meet demands beyond current government capacity.* When a government does not want to add to its permanent staff or it cannot build up its capacity quickly enough, it may turn to the private sector. This reason largely explains the interest in contracting for the operation of correctional facilities.
3. *To reduce costs.* This reason is probably the most common one for greater interest in use of the private sector, though this has been more so for local than state governments.[2]
4. *To improve service quality.* On occasion, governments may use contracts to improve service quality. States more than local governments tend to contract for this reason.
5. *To provide clients with more choice of providers and levels of service.* Some alternative service delivery approaches, such as vouchers and nonexclusive franchises, allow clients more choice regarding provider, location, and particular service characteristics. Clients usually have much more limited options if the service is provided only by public facilities.
6. *Ideology.* Some people feel that regardless of the relative costs or service quality, the less governments do, the better.

## POTENTIAL MAJOR ADVANTAGES OF PRIVATE OVER PUBLIC ORGANIZATIONS[3]

Private organizations have these important potential advantages:

1. *Less red tape and bureaucracy.* Public sector rules and regulations often hamstring public employees. A variety of rules, regulations, and procedures usually exists constraining public managers from acting quickly in the face of changing conditions. For example, it is usually easier for both for-profit and nonprofit organizations than for a government to:
   □ hire, transfer, fire, promote, reward, and even out peaks in the workload;
   □ purchase new equipment and make such purchases faster; and
   □ obtain approvals faster because of fewer layers of management.
2. *More competition.* Government agencies typically are monopo-

lies; they do not face competition. With private sector approaches such as contracting, nonexclusive franchises, and vouchers, competition can be introduced. Competition tends to motivate competing organizations to lower their prices and, if the competition is at least partly quality based, to improve service quality.[4]

3. *Lower unit costs if the private organization operates in more than one jurisdiction and can spend its investments.* Private firms that serve more than one jurisdiction can more easily justify new technical equipment, develop new management information systems, and develop and use training programs for employees. The development costs can be divided among the jurisdictions served. Multisite firms can also take advantage of economies of scale, such as by central purchasing of supplies and equipment. Because such firms may also be able to offer more opportunities for promotion to professional and management employees than can a single state department, they may attract more qualified employees.

---

## POTENTIAL MAJOR PROBLEMS WITH USE OF THE PRIVATE SECTOR

Although often acknowledged by advocates of privatization, the potential problems are sometimes treated much too casually, as if they are easy to overcome and are only minor inconveniences.

Major potential problems include: corruption, incentives to reduce the quality of service, increased chance of service interruption, and the possibility of reducing access of disadvantaged citizens to services.

1. *Potential for corruption.* When financial stakes are high, the temptations to engage in illegal actions such as bribery, kickbacks, payoffs, and fraud are great. There are many examples of surrender to these temptations, especially at the local level; the American Federation of State, County and Municipal Employees union has documented numerous instances of abuse in public sector contracting.[5] The possibility of corruption can be reduced through establishment of sound procurement procedures. Even when the government sheds direct responsibility for a service, as in divestiture or vouchers, it can institute regulations to reduce the possibility of corruption. Nevertheless, when large dollars are involved, as they are in many contracts, the potential for corruption remains an important concern.

2. *Incentives to reduce service quality.* When substantial dollars are involved, there is also a natural temptation, particularly for for-profit organizations, to do whatever is necessary to maximize profits, including skimping on quality to reduce costs. This temptation increases when a firm experiences financial difficulties, as sometimes happens even with nonprofit organizations. A classic example is lower maintenance levels that occurred when airlines have faced major financial problems.[6]

   The principal protections against poor quality are: performance and/or incentive requirements written into agreements and adequate monitoring of performance. The need for these protections has been noted by both proponents and opponents of privatization. But it is much easier to say that these protections are needed than it is to implement them effectively. Of the many government contracts that the authors have seen in recent years, most have no specific requirements regarding service quality, or they are extremely weak ones. The picture is even gloomier when one looks for systematic monitoring by agencies of service quality, whether they are monitoring contractors, service providers in voucher systems, recipients of grants, volunteers, or participants in public-private partnerships.

3. *Increased chance of service interruption.* Private organizations are more likely than governments to curtail or cease operations because of financial problems or strikes. In addition, problems may arise during the interim before a new contractor takes over. Interruptions are a particular concern when they may affect the health or safety of clients.

4. *Possible reduced access to service for the disadvantaged.* Private organizations may be tempted to avoid both clients for whom securing payment for services is likely to be difficult and those who may be particularly difficult and expensive to help—as disadvantaged clients often are. This potential applies particularly to for-profit firms, but even nonprofit private organizations are subject to the temptation.[7]

---

### SCOPE AND LIMITATIONS

This report focuses on the following selected state services:

□ corrections;
□ parks;

□ human services, including a variety of health and social services;
□ employment and training;
□ maintenance and repair of state passenger vehicles; and
□ transportation: road maintenance and drivers' and motor vehicle license services.

Our report is not a comprehensive survey of all state government agencies. Nor does it exhaust all possible opportunities for greater use of the private sector for the services covered here. For a few activities (inmate food service and maintenance of state vehicles), most states are covered comprehensively. In some instances (corrections activities and highway maintenance), we were able to use data from previous surveys of the states.

Our review focuses on recent state experiences that are less traditional applications of these alternative service delivery approaches, ones that appear significantly different from past uses. We attempted to focus on examples likely to be of interest to many states.

Exhibit 1.2 lists the examples discussed by type of service, delivery approach, and state. For more detailed information, we refer readers to the state organizations and individuals cited in the text or in the chapter endnotes.

To obtain information for this study, the authors conducted telephone interviews with staff from state agencies. We supplemented this information by examining reports and other relevant documents, such as contracts. In addition, we were able to draw on surveys previously done by us or other organizations.

Most examples of efforts had at least one year of trial. A few instances of emerging new opportunities are more recent.

In seeking examples, we did not screen out examples of failed efforts. It was not our purpose to present only success stories but to provide information on problems as well as opportunities. In fact, it was usually unclear at the beginning of a review whether the examples were success stories or not. (Unfortunately, as the reader will see, clear-cut evidence of the impacts of these experiments on costs and service quality was seldom available.) Thus, the examples described in this report represent differing degrees of success. Nevertheless, the examples likely contain some bias toward successes, if only because we were less likely to hear about trials that were considered failures and that had been discontinued.

Exhibit 1.2  PROGRAMS DESCRIBED IN THIS BOOK (page numbers)

| Service/State | Contracting | Volunteers | Vouchers | Concessions[a] | Public-Private Partnerships |
|---|---|---|---|---|---|
| *Corrections* | | | | | |
| *Food Service* | | | | | |
| Florida | 15 | | | | |
| New Mexico | 20 | | | | |
| Other states | 21 | | | | |
| *Education* | | | | | |
| Washington | 23 | | | | |
| Maryland | 25 | | | | |
| Minnesota | 26 | | | | |
| *Operation of Adult Facilities* | | | | | |
| Kentucky | 32 | | | | |
| *Parks and Recreation* | | | | | |
| Delaware | 46 | 58 | | 47 | |
| Florida | 48 | 59 | | 49 | |
| South Carolina | 50 | 60 | | 50 | |
| Virginia | 51 | 63 | | 51 | |
| Wisconsin | | | | | 53 |
| *Human Services* | | | | | |
| *Child Day Care* | | | | | |
| Massachusetts | 76 | | 76 | | |
| New Jersey | | | 78 | | |
| Pennsylvania | 79 | | | | |
| California | 81 | | | | |
| *Adoption* | | | | | |
| Illinois | | 83 | | | |
| Kentucky | 84 | | | | |
| *Dropout Prevention* | | | | | |
| Oregon | | | | | 85 |
| *Weatherization* | | | | | |
| Kansas | | | | | 87 |
| *Medicaid* | | | | | |
| Kentucky | 88 | | | | |

Exhibit 1.2 *Continued*

| Service/State | Contracting | Volunteers | Vouchers | Concessions[a] | Public-Private Partnerships |
|---|---|---|---|---|---|
| *Human Services (continued)* | | | | | |
| *Mental Retardation and Mental Health Facilities* | | | | | |
| Kentucky | 91 | | | | |
| Florida | 92, 94 | | | | |
| South Carolina | 93 | | | | |
| *Employment and Training* | | | | | |
| *Training for Displaced Workers* | | | | | |
| Illinois | | | 104 | | 104 |
| California | 105 | | | | |
| *Training for Welfare Recipients* | | | | | |
| Massachusetts | 107 | | | | 107 |
| Michigan | 109 | | | | 109 |
| Connecticut | 110 | | | | 110 |
| *Employment and Training Programs for Youth* | | | | | |
| Oregon | 112 | | | | 112 |
| *Vehicle Maintenance* | | | | | |
| New York | 124 | | | | |
| Pennsylvania | 126 | | | | |
| Ohio | 128 | | | | |
| Michigan | 130 | | | | |
| *Transportation* | | | | | |
| *Road Maintenance and Repair* | | | | | |
| California | 140 | | | | |
| Illinois | 144 | | | | |
| Iowa | 145 | | | | |
| Pennsylvania | 147 | | | | |
| District of Columbia | 150 | | | | |
| *Driver's and Vehicle Licenses* | | | | | |
| Florida | | | | | 153 |
| New Jersey | | | | | 154 |
| Minnesota | | | | | 155 |
| *Toll Bridges and Roads* | | | | | 158 |

[a]A hybrid of contracts and franchises.

In all cases, we attempted to include both a detailed description of the innovation and whatever evaluative information was available or could be readily obtained. We sought information on the impacts on cost service and service quality and on problems that arose.

We hope that states can take advantage of these experiences in deciding what to try and how best to do it.

---

### Notes

1. See, for example, Renee A. Berger, "Private Sector Initiatives in the Reagan Era: New Actors Rework an Old Theme," in *The Reagan Presidency and the Governing of America*, edited by Lester M. Salamon and Michael S. Lund (Washington, D.C.: Urban Institute Press, 1984), pp. 181–211.

2. This point is substantiated by the findings of the New Jersey State and Local Expenditure and Revenue Policy Commission,"Alternative Methods for Delivering Public Services in New Jersey," February 1987. The commission's 1986 survey of New Jersey's 21 counties and 88 municipalities found that 36 percent reported cost savings as their reason for choosing an alternative service delivery method; only 4 of 20 state departments (20 percent) that the commission surveyed mentioned cost savings as a reason.

3. For a more detailed explanation of advantages and disadvantages, the pros and cons of the individual approaches to making greater use of the private sector shown in exhibit 1.1, see Harry P. Hatry, *A Review of Private Approaches for Delivery of Public Services* (Washington, D.C.: Urban Institute Press, 1983), and E. S. Savas, *Privatization: The Key to Better Government* (Chatham, New Jersey: Chatham House, 1987).

4. State agencies, however, can stimulate improvement among their own employees, for example, by formally comparing other delivery options with state employee delivery of services or by a variety of management approaches such as improving their performance appraisal processes.

5. See, for example, John D. Hanrahan, *Government for $ale* (Washington, D.C.: American Federation of State, County and Municipal Employees, 1977).

6. The American Federation of State, County and Municipal Employees has reported many such examples associated with contracting at both the local and state government levels. See *Passing the Bucks* (Washington, D.C.: American Federation of State, County and Municipal Employees, 1983).

7. This problem has become a particular concern recently in hospital services. Episodes have been publicized in which persons without medical insurance or other funds have been turned away from private hospitals and even from emergency room care. A National Academy of Sciences study concluded that access was a major national concern, finding that for-profit hospitals served fewer uninsured patients and had a smaller percentage of uncompensated care than nonprofit hospitals. The study

also found that nonprofit hospitals provided less such care than public hospitals, although two or three times as much uncompensated care on the average as for-profit hospitals. The researchers felt that although the percentage differences were small among the types of providers, "small percentage differences, however, can translate into large numbers of patients." Bradford H. Gray, ed. *For-Profit Enterprises in Health Care* (Washington, D.C.: National Academy Press, 1986), p. 116. This "skimming" has also been noted periodically as a problem in other human service programs such as vocational rehabilitation and employment and training programs.

# Chapter Two

# USE OF THE PRIVATE SECTOR IN CORRECTIONS SERVICE DELIVERY

*Joan W. Allen*

Only a few types of approaches for greater use of the private sector are practical in the corrections field. Contracting is the primary possibility. Grants and subsidies to private organizations, volunteer help, and temporary help from private firms (e.g., soliciting donations of equipment or management advice) are also used.

A 1984 survey by Camp and Camp of contracting in correctional institutions in the 50 states found widespread contracting of support services by adult and juvenile agencies.[1] Contracting was more frequent in agencies serving juveniles than in those serving adults. Further, an average of 68 percent of agencies contracted for physical and mental health services—59 percent for operation of community treatment centers, 55 percent for basic education, and 49 percent for drug treatment.[2]

The 1984 study listed the following categories of services that corrections departments contracted for:

Aftercare
Blood Bank
Canteen, Commissary
College Programs
Community Treatment Centers
Computer Services
Construction
Counseling
Cultural Programs
Drama, Dancing
Drug Treatment
Food Service
Health Services
Hobbycraft Sales

Inmate Businesses
Laundry
Mental Health Services
Nutrition
Personnel
Physicians
Private Industry using Prison
  Labor
Recreation Therapy
Religious Programs
Security Services
Therapeutic Training for
  Inmates
Training Programs for Staff

Treatment for Sex Offenders        Vocational Programs
Transportation                     Work Release
Video Programming

Prison industries are another area of private involvement. As of 1984, 19 prison industries operated in nine states. But of the 34,000 state prison inmates participating in industry programs, fewer than 1,400 were in programs established or operated by the private sector.

This chapter first presents examples of contracting for prison services and then discusses prison volunteers and public-private partnerships. The activities discussed in the following sections are inmate food service, educational services, and operation and management of correctional facilities.

---

## CONTRACTING FOR INMATE FOOD SERVICES IN CORRECTIONAL FACILITIES

Contracts cover all or some food service activities in correctional institutions:

□ procurement,
□ warehousing,
□ transportation of food and supplies,
□ supervision of inmate meal preparation,
□ serving meals,
□ cleanup and sanitation of kitchens and dining rooms, and
□ security for kitchens and dining rooms.

Contracts vary. Some states purchase food directly or the contractor does so with state requisitions. Contractors purchase the food and include it in the contract price in other states. In some, Mississippi, for example, inmates grow food that the contractor uses along with purchased food. The states handle transportation and warehousing of food differently. Employees are usually responsible for security.

In most states that contract for food service, the contractor is completely responsible for supervision of food preparation, serving, and cleanup. In at least two states (Connecticut and Mississippi), state employees share responsibility for kitchen supervision.

A mail survey conducted by the State of Delaware found that, as of May 1987, 11 of the 40 states responding and the District of Columbia had contracted for food services at correctional facilities in the last 5 years.[3] Two of the 11 had discontinued the arrangement by 1987, although one of them was considering a small contract. Exhibit 2.1 shows data from these 11 states and the District of Columbia.

Most requests for proposals (RFPs) and contracts for food services examined were written for one or two years and were fairly general except that they required a minimum number of calories per day per inmate and allowed for special dietary needs. The price per meal was usually about $1.10, depending on what work the contract covered and how much food the inmates grew.

The corrections food services contracting experiences of Florida and New Mexico, both having detailed contractual arrangements, are presented below.

### Florida

*DESCRIPTION*

Florida experienced difficulty hiring competent employees to supervise food services, especially for facilities in areas with high average wages for people trained in food services. The state paid about $16,000 annually plus benefits to employees with the job classification of "food service." Correctional officials had to use regular correctional officers to supervise food services. These employees were paid more than $20,000 plus benefits. When these services were contracted for, the state employees were transferred to jobs other than food services. Contract food services employees were paid about $21,000, but with fewer fringe benefits than the state provided. A regional food services director for the contractor received about $28,000.

Contractors feed about 3,800 inmates and 150 staff in four of the 32 major correctional facilities and in one state hospital. The contractors (one for the four major correctional facilities and the other for hospitalized prisoners) are responsible for procurement of all food, meal preparation for inmates and staff, serving inmates and staff, and cleanup. The food is delivered directly to each facility,

Exhibit 2.1   STATE DEPARTMENTS OF CORRECTIONS THAT CONTRACT FOR FOOD SERVICES

| State | First year contract | Number inmate meals/day | Cost/ meal | Scope of contract | Cost[a] | Quality[a] | Staff provided meals | Comments | Contractor[b] |
|---|---|---|---|---|---|---|---|---|---|
| Arkansas | 1978 | 775 | $3.00 | Meal preparation for inmates | Much higher | About same | No | State hospital prepares food for inmates housed there | State hospital |
| Connecticut | 1983 | 2,700 | $0.73–$0.84 | Procurement, transportation, warehousing | About same | About same | No | Contractor shares responsibility with state supervisors | Canteen/Szabo |
| District of Columbia | 1982 | 4,200 | $1.80 | Meal preparation, procurement, transportation, warehousing | Somewhat higher | About same | No | Contracted to try to reduce costs; having trouble keeping staff | Canteen/Marriott |
| Florida | 1985 | 9,453 | $1.00–$1.35 | Meal preparation, procurement | Somewhat higher | Somewhat better | Yes | Unusually good specs in RFP | Service America |
| Idaho | Early 1980 | — | — | — | Higher | Lower | — | DOC very dissatisfied with entire operation, contractor | Szabo |

Exhibit 2.1 Continued

| State | Year | Number | Cost | Services | Cost comparison | Quality | | Comments | Contractor |
|---|---|---|---|---|---|---|---|---|---|
| Illinois | 1981 | 3,750 | $1.09 | Meal preparation, procurement, transportation, warehousing | Somewhat lower | Somewhat better | Yes | Good specs in RFP | Szabo Servomation |
| Indiana | — | 160 | — | Meal preparation, procurement, transportation, warehousing | Much higher | Somewhat worse | Yes | Includes 100 work release, 60 juveniles; plan to discontinue | — |
| Minnesota | 1975 | 5,010 | $1.00 | Meal preparation, procurement, transportation, warehousing | Unknown | Better | Yes | Local company, very satisfied | Best, Inc. |
| Mississippi | 1981 | 15,900 | $1.13 | Meal preparation, procurement, transportation, warehousing | Much lower | Somewhat better | Yes | State dieticians share some responsibility for food service | Szabo/Morrison |
| New Mexico | 1985 | 3,600 | $1.59 | Meal procurement, transportation, warehousing | About same | Somewhat better | Yes | Contracted because of difficulty staffing | Canteen/Service America/Szabo |

(continued)

Exhibit 2.1 Continued

| State | First year contract | Number inmate meals/day | Cost/ meal | Scope of contract | Cost[a] | Quality[a] | Staff provided meals | Comments | Contractor[b] |
|---|---|---|---|---|---|---|---|---|---|
| Oklahoma | Early 1980s | 3,900 | $0.74 | Meal procurement, transportation, warehousing | Higher | Worse | No | Contractor "inexperienced"; state considering contracting again | ARA |
| West Virginia | 1984 | 3,150 | — | Meal preparation includes 550 staff | Much lower | Much better | Yes | Contracted to cut costs, use different contractors at two institutions | Canteen and American Food Management/Service America and AFM/ Morrison |

Source: Delaware Department of Corrections, "Report on Service Alternatives for Food Services," Smyrna, 21 May 1987.
[a]Compared to state run.
[b]Most recent vendor listed first.

eliminating warehousing. Inmates help prepare and serve food for both inmates and staff. The contractor provides three meals per day.

The price per inmate meal varied with each contract: $1.00, $1.01, $1.03, and $1.33, as of spring 1987, for the four basic contracts. The latter price is expected to drop when the contract is rebid. (It was higher than the others because the kitchen at a new facility was not finished and the contractor had to do the cooking at another location.) The cost is supposed to be adjusted each year according to the consumer price index. In fact, it has dropped some because of competition for the contract.

The contractor follows menus prescribed by the Department of Corrections dietician, a typical provision in food service contracts. The contractor pays inmates 20–25 cents per hour for their work. Where food services are not contracted for, the state pays inmates more per hour, but subsistence is deducted from their wages; the wages are comparable.

Food service contractors must provide 40 hours of training for each inmate and for each contractor employee working in food service. The state food services coordinator believes that outside employees need more training than is required in both food service techniques and relations with inmates.[4]

*ASSESSMENT*

The state food services coordinator reported that the quality of the food was better under the contract arrangement because it did not have to be ordered four months in advance, as in the state procurement process, and seasonal bargains add variety. The coordinator also felt that vendors tend to supply the state with poorer quality food than they supply to private contractors.

Contracted meals at one correctional facility were estimated by the state to have cost somewhat more than at a comparable facility with state-run food service (3 cents more than one year, 15 cents more another)—but the price is expected to decrease when the contract is rebid. According to the state food services coordinator, the state saves money by eliminating the multiple steps of state procurement, and the need for warehousing food. These factors may not have been given full weight in cost comparisons.

The coordinator also noted that cleanliness and sanitation of the kitchens improved "100 percent" since contracting.

**New Mexico**

*DESCRIPTION*

Because the Department of Corrections could not find personnel who were both good cooks and good managers, it turned to contracting in 1984. (Nationwide contractors have the advantage of selecting personnel from all over the country.)

As a result, contractors now feed about 1,200 inmates and 500 staff in three of the state's seven adult facilities. The state uses one-year contracts that permit annual renewals without rebidding if the state is satisfied with contractor performance. New Mexico is not required to rebid the contract after a specific number of years; however, a state official supervising food services said that it probably would do so after "two or three years" because it would reduce the advantages of competition to renew the same company's contract automatically too many times. In practice, New Mexico has had three contractors in as many years.[5]

The contractor is responsible for procurement, transportation, warehousing, preparation and serving both inmates and staff, and cleanup and sanitation. Each facility prepares three meals a day.

The performance of the first contractor was unsatisfactory. A new RFP was more specific than the first, but the second contractor performed unsatisfactorily. Under an even more specific RFP, a third contractor is rated satisfactory.

The prison official supervising food services said that he had learned a lot by writing three successive RFPs on the quality of protein provided daily, on the meats served on summer and winter holidays, and, for casseroles, the exact proportions in which they may be combined.[6] State food services contracts now specify minimum USDA grades for different categories of food.

The contractor is now required to submit questionnaires on the *quality* of food service to the inmates every three months. As a benefit to inmates, the contractor must provide inmate vocational training in food preparation and basic cooking. (West Virginia requires contractors to provide inmate classes that may eventually be certified for vocational education credit.)

Fewer than half the public employees displaced by contracts went to work for the first contractor. The others, given the opportunity to become correctional officers, did not protest the contracting.

*ASSESSMENT*

A major characteristic of New Mexico's contracting for corrections food service is the increase in performance requirements added to RFPs as the state gained experience with the contracts. Contractor performance improved as RFPs became tighter.

No formal cost comparisons have been made between contracting and state-run employee food services at correctional facilities. The supervising official suspects that contracting is somewhat more expensive than state delivery but much less cumbersome—and less of a headache to state administrators. The official also noted the comparative ease with which a contractor can obtain bargains on food.

The state contracts supervisor believes that food services have improved somewhat with contracting. Apparently, no inmates or staff had grievances about the food services in the past year. The official also stated that a constant vigil must be kept on cleanliness, whether food services are delivered by public employees or a contractor. The current contractor has performed satisfactorily in this area.

### Problems in Other States that Contract for Food Services

In at least two states, Mississippi and Connecticut, state supervisors *shared responsibility* for food services with contractors. A Connecticut corrections official indicated that this split responsibility can cause major problems in the delivery of food services because public and private supervisors sometimes vie for final authority.[7] In Connecticut, the state supervisors and the private managers are in the kitchens at all times. Mississippi indicated no problems with shared responsibility. In 1983 and 1984, Oklahoma contracted for food services to 1,300 inmates at two correctional institutions. In late 1984, inmates at one of them burned down the facility, primarily to protest poor meals. The food services contract was immediately canceled. About seven times as many inmate grievances on food services had been received under contracting than under state operation, according to a corrections official.[8] However, Oklahoma is again considering a small corrections food services RFP.[9]

**Summary of Findings and Recommendations on Food Service Contracting**

Exhibit 2.1 tabulates information on food services contracts in 11 states and the District of Columbia.
The major findings were:

1. Many states had difficulty finding competent food service workers willing to work for state salaries. This consideration was a major impetus to contracting for food service.
2. A major advantage of contracting food services is that it removes the headache of supervising the services, felt to be somewhat peripheral to basic corrections work.
3. Six of the 12 governments reported that food quality was better after contracting. In three, food service quality dropped after contracting, and two of the three discontinued contracting. The remaining three governments felt that quality was "about the same" under contractors.
4. Detailed comparisons of food service costs before and after contracting were not possible, partly because the states do not keep detailed cost records and partly because the contractors' responsibilities for components of food services varied from state to state.
5. The states reported little formal evaluation of their contractors. The states seemed content to go along with contracting once it began, provided that costs did not escalate and that complaints about quality were few.
6. Both states that stopped contracting for food services, Oklahoma and Idaho, did not adequately monitor the contractors' performance. One of the states was considering a small contract at one institution to see whether contracting would work with more careful monitoring.

Some insights gained by studying contracting for food services at state correctional institutions are:

☐ The state RFPs should specify in detail such requirements as the minimum amount of meat per week (to avoid the use of too much protein substitute) and the menu for certain holidays. New Mexico, as discussed earlier, learned to write more detail into each of three successive RFPs.
☐ The states must closely monitor the contracted delivery of food services. Inmate and staff complaints should be conveyed

promptly to the central state office responsible for contractor performance.

☐ Dividing responsibility for parts of food services between state employees and contractors is probably risky.

☐ Large contractors can recruit employees from a larger, usually nationwide pool of qualified applicants. Further, contract employees who are specialists may be more efficient than public employees who are less knowledgeable about food services.

---

## CONTRACTING FOR EDUCATION IN CORRECTIONAL INSTITUTIONS

The 1984 Camp and Camp survey cited earlier found that 23 states and the District of Columbia, or 47 percent of the jurisdictions studied, contracted for some type of education in their correctional facilities.[10] The authors interviewed education directors for Corrections Departments in six of these states: Connecticut, Florida, Maryland, Minnesota, Virginia, and Washington. To assess alternative service delivery in Maryland, we also met with several corrections officials involved in inmate education. The following sections describe contracting in Washington, Maryland, and Minnesota, for which we have the most detailed information.

### Washington[11]

#### DESCRIPTION

To our knowledge, Washington is the only state that contracts *all* education services in its correctional facilities.

Washington phased in contracting for these services after a 1977 audit criticized the coordination and management by state employees. The report summarized well the arguments for contracting educational services in correctional institutions. It stated:

The tie with an educational institution strengthens liaison and cooperation with the entire educational community. This argument can be expanded to specific advantages which include (1) ease of locating and hiring teachers with specific skills, either full or part-time, (2) access to assorted resources on a loan or temporary basis, specifically including audio-visual equipment and training aids, and (3) a degree of continuity can be maintained in the education/training program when an institutional resident is dis-

charged and desires to continue his education/training program. Credits
are readily transferable. . . .
Finally, it is eloquently argued that contracted education and training programs result in a written commitment of funds to education and training. . . . In summary, institutions without contractual commitments found
it irresistable to raid the Education and Training Program budget as a
means of resolving any unforeseen emergency or unanticipated expense
which might be encountered.[12]

By 1982, inmate education was *entirely* contracted for in the
state of Washington. All contracts in Washington are with nonprofit
institutions. Contracts with for-profit institutions are legally allowed, but there is an unwritten understanding between the Department of Corrections and the legislature that for-profit
educational contractors will be approached only if public institutions cannot supply the services needed. This agreement is pre-
sumed to assuage public school teachers who want to keep the
responsibility they have in corrections education. Contracts have
been with public community colleges and public vocational-technical institutes; they currently total approximately $5.5 million.

The corrections department has established an advisory committee consisting of representatives of business, industry, and labor
and of other citizens for each vocational-technical program offered
in state correctional institutions. The committees advise on curric-
ulum and are a conduit for donations of equipment and job placement assistance for inmates.

### ASSESSMENT

The Washington corrections department had performed no evaluation of the quality and cost of educational services in correctional
facilities delivered by contractors compared to those delivered by
public employees, but the director of education believes that the
1977 mandate of the legislature is being fulfilled.

The Department of Corrections, in a report to the legislature in
1981, seemed to acknowledge the need for closer monitoring:

Greater emphasis has been placed [this year] on educational program review and monitoring than in previous contracts. The newly appointed
Educational Administrator for the Department of Corrections will take an
active role in not only monitoring the educational programs but also monitoring the terms of the contract.[13]

## Maryland

*DESCRIPTION*

The State of Maryland contracts with Hagerstown Junior College for instruction at three correctional facilities in and near Hagerstown. The contract covers vocational courses in clerical work, construction trades, automotive and power service, and wood and metal manufacturing and fabrication trades, plus some employment counseling for youths.[14] The contract was not competitively bid; corrections officials decided to try contracting with a nearby college whose facilities were familiar to them. The contract is in fact written with the Maryland Department of Education, not the Department of Corrections.

The contract for September 1986 through June 1987 specified the number of hours of instruction for men at three Hagerstown facilities. Instruction was billed at $9.50 per hour. The college was also responsible for providing a specified number of hours of work by two paraprofessionals in job counseling at $5.98 an hour and for vocational counseling and placement. For each service, dollar maximums were specified. Equipment and tools for the classes taught by Hagerstown Junior College employees are provided by the Department of Corrections.[15]

*ASSESSMENT*

The college is heavily subsidized by federal and state governments. A corrections department work group discovered in a cost analysis that the Department of Corrections saved money by contracting for these courses even though some teachers received higher salaries than do state employees of the Department of Education in similar jobs at Maryland prisons.[16]

Corrections education officials agreed that the quality of the college teaching at least equaled that of state employees, some of whom still teach at the Hagerstown facilities. They also felt that contracting allowed much more *flexibility* in adapting courses to new techniques in vocational education and in changing courses as different kinds of skills are needed in current job markets. It was much easier to change vocational courses in response to changing technology and variations in the job market by contracting with vocational teachers outside the state education system than it is to try to hire, transfer, fire, or promote for changes within the state civil service system.[17]

### Minnesota[18]

*DESCRIPTION*

Contracts for a part of corrections education in Minnesota were first let about 12 years ago. Although the current education director was not involved then, he believes that the principal motivation was the flexibility afforded by contracting compared to dealing with the state civil service system when making changes to establish, revise, or cancel courses. It is not clear how the choices were made originally as to which courses would be taught by state employees and which would be contracted for, but it was probably on a course-by-course and institution-by-institution basis.

At two adult institutions, all vocational education is contracted for: five courses at one facility but only two (computer programming and drafting) at the other. At the Willow River facility, the contracted courses include welding, machine tool, truck driving, mechanics, and truck and trailer repair. At Stillwater, a state employee teaches welding; carpentry, carpenter's aide, horticulture, and machine shop courses are contracted for. Vocational courses at Minnesota's other correctional facilities are taught by state employees, with one exception. At a new women's prison at Shakopee, contractors have taught a 3-week nurse's assistant course and a 10-week landscaping course. A nearby public vocational school is working with the new prison to develop a two-way television link between the two institutions.

All college-level courses at state correctional facilities are contracted for. State employees teach 75 percent of adult basic education courses in state prisons. The remaining 25 percent are taught by part-time individual tutors with whom the state contracts. Approximately 13 percent of the state corrections education budget, or $734,000, goes to contractors. The entire budget totals about $5.5 million.[19]

A consortium of six schools, including four colleges, a small university, and a public vocational-technical (voc-tech) school, is the contractor for all education at one facility. The contract covers instruction in basic skills, including preparation for the General Educational Development (GED) program, a full-time college program, vocational courses, an art program, and other short courses.[20]

Only contracts for college courses and what the consortium offers are competitive. Voc-tech contracts are not let through RFPs except for those courses taught by the consortium. The other voc-tech contracts are all held by nonprofits: a local public school, two colleges, and one voc-tech school.

Under a special agreement, Rasmussen College, a private institution, offers a small business management course at one correctional facility at no charge to the state. The college receives federal Pell Grant funds to cover its costs and profit. Rasmussen provides instruction, support personnel, equipment, and materials to conduct the course within state guidelines set by the Minnesota Department of Education and the Accreditation Commission of Independent Schools and Colleges. Although the state is satisfied with the quality of the Rasmussen program, it is not actively seeking additional similar arrangements.

### ASSESSMENT

No cost comparisons have been made between contracting and using public employees for corrections education in Minnesota. The principal advantage to contracting for vocational courses seems to be its flexibility in revising courses in accord with changing technology and a changing job market, the same conclusion reached in Maryland.[21] Further, no formal comparison has been made of the quality of teaching by public employees versus contracted employees. One official believes that the state does not encourage more competitive bidding for contracting because, due to geography and weather, the state deems it good practice to make arrangements with colleges and vocational schools near each institution. Apparently, once a contract is awarded, it is virtually impossible to get other potential vendors to bid on it when it comes up for renewal.

The state's increasing the amount of contracting for educational services in the near future was thought to be unlikely. Some directors of prison facilities were adamantly against contracting, and the state does not urge them to try it.

### Summary of Findings and Recommendations on Contracting for Educational Services in Correctional Facilities

The issue of flexibility in changing courses and instructors to keep up with technology and the job market emerged as a theme during interviews with corrections education officials. Officials seem to agree that contracting for vocational instruction makes it much easier to be flexible than dealing with state employees under civil service restrictions. Officials believe that the quality of instruction under contract and that delivered by state employees are similar. Except for Maryland, the states had no cost comparisons between public employee and contract employee services.

Competition has not been widely used for corrections education. Even less used has been competition involving for-profit firms. It may be that with increasing use of computer-aided instruction, a field in which for-profit firms have done the most work, these firms will be allowed to compete in the future.

## *CONTRACTING FOR THE OPERATION OF ENTIRE CORRECTIONAL INSTITUTIONS*

Correctional institutions are for adults or for juveniles and they are secure or nonsecure. Although correctional agencies do not always agree on what constitutes different levels of security, secure institutions generally have one or more of the following features: razor wire fences; high walls; mobile patrols; detection devices (e.g., TV cameras or high-mast lighting); and, in the case of maximum security facilities, gun towers. Facilities considered nonsecure usually have no fences or patrols.

Contracting and the use of grants or subsidies are prevalent ways of providing *juvenile* programs for secure and, particularly, nonsecure facilities. In Massachusetts, for example, of 12 secure juvenile *treatment* facilities listed in a Department of Youth Services document, 5 were privately operated. Of 8 secure *detention* (i.e., short-term) youth programs, 3 were privately operated. However, all but 1 nonsecure shelter care program and all nonsecure group care programs for juveniles in Massachusetts were privately operated.[22]

Private companies and organizations operate *secure juvenile* facilities in several states, including Pennsylvania, Tennessee, Massachusetts, and Florida.

Overcrowding has become a major problem in U.S. correctional institutions. Four factors contributed to this crisis in providing and managing enough prison space.[23]

□ demographics (a population bulge of 18- to 25-year-olds, the age group most likely to be incarcerated),
□ expansion of inmate rights (prisons cannot remain overcrowded),
□ society's demands for tougher sentencing policies for criminals, and
□ increased fiscal constraints on government.

Federal court orders to relieve overcrowding and the states' need to reduce costs have moved the states to consider allowing private operators to run state prisons. Frustration with an often ineffective and inefficient correctional system is also a "powerful motive" for such innovation.[24] One author noted:

The federal courts will not permit the State [of Tennessee] to continue its past practices [of overcrowding and mistreatment] and have ordered major reforms to bring the prison system within constitutional limits. Facilities must be built or renovated, new educational and vocational programs implemented, and a host of other problems corrected before the federal courts will relinquish oversight.[25]

Court orders on other states are similar.

The states, as well as other levels of government, have begun looking at alternative ways to finance, build, and manage correctional institutions. Although this chapter does not examine the financing and buildings of prisons, it is worth noting that in July 1986 Southeast Missouri Correctional Facility, Inc., a private firm, issued more than $55 million in tax-exempt bonds to finance the construction of a 500-bed prison in Potosi, Missouri. The prison, which is to be financed, built, and operated by private firms, will be leased to the state for 30 years for payments of $4.5 million per year. At the end of the 30 years, Missouri will own the prison.

A private firm created detailed plans for putting a compact prison of less than 35 acres on the site of a large inactive industrial park. The cost of building the prison is less than the state had estimated, and the design is expected to save on maintenance. State officials estimate that the private sector will trim two years off construction time.[26]

Many nonsecure halfway houses and similar facilities for adults are operated by private vendors, but until the past few years, there has been little contracting for secure facilities for *adults*. No private vendor operates a *maximum* security facility for adults.

The sections below include information on contracted *local* government corrections facilities.

As of early 1987, approximately 1,100 adults were held in minimum security correctional facilities that were privately operated for state or local governments in the United States.[27] These institutions include:

☐ State of Kentucky: Marion Adjustment Center, 200 men, minimum security, for-profit contractor;
☐ State of Florida: Beckham Hall Community Correctional Center, Miami, 171 men, unsupervised work release, for-profit contractor;
☐ Bay County, Florida: Jail and annex, 350 men and women, for-profit contractor;
☐ Hamilton County, Tennessee (Chattanooga): Silverdale Detention Center, workhouse, 340 men and women, for-profit contractor; and
☐ Ramsey County, Minnesota (St. Paul): Roseville Detention Center, 42 women, nonprofit operator.

All contracts except the one for Minnesota are with for-profit vendors; Volunteers of America operates the Roseville Center.

In addition to the above facilities, two state prerelease facilities in Texas are to be built and operated by private contractors. Two private companies selected in October 1987 will each build and operate two 500-inmate prerelease facilities in Texas, for a total of 2,000 beds. The state had closed the doors to its prison system more than 20 times during 1987, when the population topped the limit of 95 percent of the number of beds available.[28] The two private companies were among six finalists chosen from 19 bidders.

Private prisons, authorized in Texas in 1987, are limited to 2,000 beds for at least the first two years. The state plans to build and operate at least four 1,000-bed prerelease centers and two 2,250-bed maximum security prisons by 1989.

Hopes for contracting complete prison operation include those of the Tennessee Department of Corrections. In 1986, the state issued an RFP for operation of a medium-security prison but received no responsive bids. The department has been considering revision and reissue of the RFP.

Contract lengths for currently contracted facilities range from 1 year (Ramsey County) to 20 years (Bay County). The vendor in Bay County, Corrections Corporation of America, also rehabilitated the jail and built a large annex. The Bay County Jail becomes county property for a payment of one dollar ($1) after the 20 years.[29] The Hamilton County contract is for four years, but it can be renewed up to seven times without rebidding it. The contract calls for major renovation as well as operation of facilities. If the county terminates the contract, it is liable for all capital improvements that the contractor has made at the facility.[30]

All the contracts for adult inmates listed provided for payment on a per diem basis, ranging (in 1987) from $20.81 at Beckham Hall, Florida, a work release center, to $56.75 for those women inmates at Roseville, Minnesota who did not go out on work release. It is standard for the contract price to be renegotiated annually, usually taking into consideration the cost of living index for the area where the prison is located.

A major issue in contracting for facility operation is what specific activities the contractor will be responsible for.

Basic *medical care* is customarily listed as the responsibility of the contractor, with emergency care and hospitalization costs to be paid by the state. The Bay County contract was not specific on this point, and there was prolonged negotiation before the state agreed to pay for emergency medical care and visits to medical specialists outside the prison.

Responsibility for *transportation* for prisoners varies from contract to contract, but contractors are normally responsible for transportation for medical purposes.

Contracts often spell out the physical requirements for *security* at the prisons, and they usually specify the level of force that the staff may use. The Bay County contract is typical. It calls for the contractor to have a "written policy and procedure restricting the use of physical force by staff to instances of justifiable self-protection, protection of others, protection of property and prevention of escapes and only to the degree necessary. Following all use of force, a full written report shall be submitted to Bay County's Contract Monitor." The contract also calls for "provisions for all staff to be trained in emergency preparedness and responses, i.e., hostage taking, riot and disturbance, fire, work stoppage, etc." The Hamilton County, Tennessee contract has similar provisions.[31] At Beckham Hall, the use of force may be employed "only as a last resort" and in accordance with Florida law. The RFP for the Marion, Kentucky facility, incorporated into the contract, states that "[t]he center shall have a written policy restricting the use of physical force to instances of justifiable self-protection, prevention of property damage and prevention of escapes, and only to the degree necessary and in accordance with appropriate statutory authority.[32] The use of force by staff is not mentioned in the Roseville contract for the women's detention and work release facility.

### Kentucky Marion Adjustment Center

Experience at the Marion Adjustment Center illustrates some of the benefits and problems in contracting for operation of corrections facilities.

*DESCRIPTION*

The State of Kentucky was under court order to reduce prison overcrowding by the early 1980s. It wanted to avoid the lengthy state process for acquiring or building facilities. In 1984, the state issued an RFP for a 200-bed minimum security facility for adult men. All proposals exceeded the Corrections Department budget for the facility; the budget for the facility had not been publicized, so the state issued a second RFP.[33] A small company, Bannum, won the contract with a proposal based on the purchase of a site formerly used by International Harvester in Louisville, Kentucky. But the community resisted this plan, so the contract was awarded to the company in second place, U.S. Corrections Corporation.

U.S. Corrections had already acquired a former seminary in a rural area of Kentucky for the prison. It paid for acquisition and renovation of the site. The contract term was November 1985 to November 1988, with an option for two one-year extensions. The contract contains no performance incentives or penalties.[34] U.S. Corrections is responsible for complete management and operation of the correctional facility, keeping detailed inmate records as specified by the state and reporting "incidents" (e.g., escapes and riots) to the state. Except for initial transfer of inmates to the center, the contractor is responsible for all transportation of inmates, including transportation to and from medical appointments, parole board hearings, disciplinary returns to other correctional facilities, vocational and educational programs, and community work projects.[35]

The contractor is authorized to recommend award for "meritorious time" to be taken off an inmate's sentence for good behavior. Final approval of such awards, however, rests with the state Corrections Cabinet.[36] The contract does not provide for a minimum law library for inmates, an omission that caused friction between the state and the contractor.

U.S. Corrections was able to house prisoners almost immediately because it had acquired a facility even before bidding. The company had originally planned to use abandoned hospital buildings in Louisville, but community opposition prevents its doing so. Community opposition near Marion was also high, but when the company hired several residents of nearby Lebanon for the prison staff, opposition diminished.

The facility accepted its first inmate in January 1986. Filling it to the stated capacity of 200 was difficult because the state transferred only the cream of the crop—inmates that were judged least likely to cause any trouble.

The fee charged by U.S. Corrections was lowered through continued negotiation from an originally proposed $44.44 per inmate day to $25 in the final contract.[37] The per diem as of December 1987 was $25.35, raised in accord with the consumer price index, as the original RFP provided.

One factor that helped the state bring down the fee was its listing of actual costs at comparable state-run facilities. (The original winning vendor, Bannum, had proposed charging only $17 per day.) As U.S. Corrections gradually reduced its charges, it also reduced the size of the staff that it proposed to use.

In its first few months of operation, the prison experienced more escapes than comparable state-run facilities did, but there was only one escape for March–December 1987 after the facility had been in operation for about one year.[38] The state waived a condition of the original RFP and contract that the perimeter of the facility be fenced and guarded with dogs. The contractor gave the seven or eight families living nearest the prison radios on which they are warned when a prisoner escapes.[39]

One problem that surfaced early at Marion was the contract's failure to cover responsibility for certain activities; a minimum law library for inmates was mentioned above. The contract omitted other small-cost issues, such as paying for training the private firm's security officers. The lack of a law library made it necessary for prisoners to be transferred to state-operated facilities for any major disciplinary hearings. The contractor has since purchased law books for a minimum library. In addition, a Marion inmate was temporarily transferred to another institution to receive training in paralegal work and then returned to Marion to assist inmates in preparing their defenses for disciplinary hearings.

Because the Marion facility is in a rural area with less opportunity for work release, educational and vocational programs exceed the average for minimum security facilities in Kentucky.[40]

The contractor is monitored by an on-site state employee who also serves as a regional probation officer for the state. Long-term performance will be evaluated by a team from the central state office of the Kentucky Department of Corrections.

### ASSESSMENT

U.S. Corrections officials said after five months of operation that the company was losing money on the contract in the short term, but they hoped to make a profit in the long run.

Kentucky did not plan to evaluate the quality or the cost of the service at Marion until the contract was in its second year. As of November 1987, no evaluations had been released by the state.

#### Other Problems at Contracted Facilities

Problems that surfaced at other facilities may provide valuable insights for those who will be writing contracts.

In Bay County, Florida and Hamilton County, Tennessee there was considerable unrest among state employees when it was first rumored, then announced, that the state was going to turn over operation of the correctional facilities to private contractors. In both cases, the contractor hired all state employees who wished to switch to private employment. Most of the employees stayed at the facility in Bay County, but in Tennessee more than half had left within a year or so after the contractor took over operation of the facility. It should be noted that for other reasons, Tennessee employees were unhappy prior to contracting.

A group of citizens supporting the county sheriff, who did not want his jail taken over by a private contractor, sued Bay County for violating inmates' rights, but the protest did not prevail in court. In Bay County there was also confusion about division of responsibilities between the state and the contractor for transportation and medical treatment. The medical dispute was settled only after prolonged negotiations.

#### Summary of Findings and Recommendations on Contracting for Entire Facilities

The following recommendations are based on information compiled by The Urban Institute and The Council of State Governments from contracts and other documents and interviews with state officials and private operators.[41]

1. *Feasibility of contracting*. States facing considerable overcrowding, often resulting in court orders to remedy the situation,
   should consider contracting. Particularly in building new facilities, when a contractor can often avoid much red tape and complete buildings much faster than a state, contracting may seem
   to be an ideal solution to the state's problems. But states should
   undertake systematic, detailed analyses to determine whether,
   and under what conditions, contracting is likely to be helpful in
   their corrections systems. Their analyses should include:
   □ an examination of whether statutory authority exists,
   □ current state prison costs and the status of crowding and per-
     formance,
   □ the legal issues involved,
   □ availability of suppliers (to assure competition for a contract),
   □ discussion of whether both nonprofit and for-profit groups
     should be allowed to bid,
   □ ways to reduce the likelihood and consequences of contractor
     defaults, and
   □ consideration of the attitudes of various interest groups to-
     ward contracting for corrections operations.
   If a state's goal in contracting is to obtain new beds quickly, the
   private sector offers an attractive alternative. However, if the
   main goal is a more economical operation, the minimal evidence available to date suggests that contracting does not necessarily save a significant amount of money.
      For new institutions, contracting entails fewer problems (e.g.,
   personnel problems) than it does when an existing facility is
   turned over to a private firm; thus contracting should be given
   preference for new facilities.
2. *Cost comparisons*. When making cost comparisons, state officials should remember that many variables relate to cost: age
   and design of a facility, security level and custody needs, population size and homogeneity, sentence lengths and turnover,
   variety and types of programs, and details of capital financing.[42]
3. *Inmate rights*. Contracts should provide adequate protection of
   the inmates' rights and protect the state from unjust liability
   claims. The state can reduce but not eliminate its vulnerability
   to lawsuits when contracting by specifying in the contract that
   the state is indemnified against any damage award and for the
   cost of litigation.
4. *Contracting process*. The states should use competitive bidding
   for contracting. This process avoids accusations of cronyism
   and fraud and tends to reduce vendors' bids.

To maximize the number of bidders, a state can:

☐ advertise in major state newspapers and the national corrections journals,

☐ develop and maintain a list of potential bidders, and

☐ permit both in-state and out-of-state private nonprofit and for-profit organizations to bid.

The RFP should include information about the bid evaluation process. Suggested evaluation criteria include, but are not limited to:

☐ experience and success in similar undertakings,

☐ staff qualifications,

☐ management capability,

☐ proposed programs,

☐ financial condition and references, and

☐ price.

A method for resolving any contractual differences that may emerge should be agreed to and specified in the contract before it is activated.

5. *Contract provisions.* The RFPs and subsequent contracts should explicitly state: (a) who is responsible for which expenditures and (b) what levels of performance are expected, including compliance with minimum standards for particular policies, procedures, and practices; results on such performance indicators as maximum numbers of various "extraordinary occurrences"; and compliance with fire, safety, medical, health, and sanitation standards. The RFPs and contracts should also identify sanctions or penalties that will apply for inadequate performance. The contract should specify what reports and access it will provide to the state for its own monitoring process (as discussed below).

A tiered fee, or variable price structure, that is fair to both parties should be built into the contract to avoid future misunderstandings regarding cost for vacant beds and/or additional inmates beyond the specified ceiling.

Rebidding should occur approximately every three years. State laws and regulations should be checked before including this requirement because they may specify different maximum lengths for contracts.

Contracts should require contractors to give advance notice of the end of a union contract, the probable onset of labor difficulties, or major workers grievances that could result in a work stoppage or slowdown.

The state should consider requiring that a significant perform-ance bond be posted or a trust fund established to indemnify it in the event of a contractor's financial or other problems. The state should first determine whether the protection is worth the cost of the bond.

6. *Public employee protections.* States writing contracts that will displace state employees should take steps to avoid problems with state personnel, including:
   □ requiring the contractor to give employment preference to displaced public employees;
   □ providing for transfer, retraining, and outplacement services to public employees choosing not to work for the contractor; and
   □ calculating carefully and providing for disposition of benefits (especially retirement and vacation/sick leave accrual) to pub-lic employees.

7. *Selection of inmates.* Both the RFP and the subsequent contract should be explicit in describing the type and level of offenders to be incarcerated and the major architectural features necessary to confine the prisoners. The contract should be based on the state's current inmate classification policy and its operational definitions of the privileges and level of supervision to be ac-corded the type of inmates at the proposed custody level.

   The contract should obligate the vendor to accept all prison-ers in certain categories (e.g., minimum security) for the dura-tion of the contract period, up to the specified maximum number of inmates to be incarcerated at any given time. This provision protects the state against the possibility of selective acceptance by the contractor.

   Selection of inmates for placement in a private facility and decisions about their movement are the state's responsibility. The contract should state bases for these selections, thus avoid-ing misunderstandings.

   To facilitate planning and cost estimates, the contract should state both a minimum and maximum prisoner population level. The contract should permit the state to reassign or reclassify inmates when contractual capacity is reached.

   States contracting for large institutions may want to specify in the RFPs and the contracts that the selected private vendors can use unit management—that is, can divide the total number of beds into smaller, semiautonomous units.

8. *Disciplinary and release decision responsibilities.* State officials

should ensure that disciplinary hearings conducted by the contractor follow legally required practices. A private firm should
adopt the policies and procedures customarily used by the government doing the contracting. Significant disciplinary actions
should be formally approved by the state. Private contractor dis-
cretionary actions involving inmate rights and discipline
should require ratification by the appropriate state agency or official. These elements should be spelled out in the contract.

The state should consider permanently stationing one or more
of its own staff members at large private facilities (i.e., 150 inmates or more); at least, it should provide for frequent monitoring visits. The monitor's responsibilities would include
participation in all disciplinary hearings concerning major rule
infractions, described in written policy statements.

In the event of an escape attempt, private prison employees
should use reasonable and appropriate restraint in the absence
of specific statutory or case law. Once an inmate has left the
facility's property (unless the private prison employees are in
pursuit or have been deputized), state or local state law enforce-
ment officials become responsible for the ultimate capture and
return of the escapee.

Although individual practices may differ regarding the degree
of involvement of the public correctional agency with release
decisions, the private sector's contribution to this process
should be limited to a presentation of the facts pertaining to the
inmate's level of adjustment during the period of confinement
in the private facility. Public officials should make the decision.

9. *Monitoring.* The state should plan (before the RFP is issued) and
   implement (after the contract is awarded) an effective system for
   continuous contract monitoring. This system should include:
   - regular on-site inspections (at least monthly and preferably
     weekly) using checklists, rating categories, and guidelines on
     how to complete the ratings;
   - regular timely reports (showing tabulations and analyses of
     extraordinary occurrences, other significant performance in-
     dicators, and the results of on-site inspections);
   - periodic documented fire, safety, health and medical, and
     sanitation inspections;
   - regular interviews with samples of inmates to obtain feedback
     on performance elements such as treatment of prisoners,
     amount of internal security, drug use, and helpfulness and
     adequacy of educational, work, and recreational programs;
   - annual in-depth on-site inspections by a team of experts cov-

ering procedures and periodic reports on the facility's quality of services based on precontract specified results indicators;
□ explicit provision in the department's procedures for prompt review by state officials of the written findings from each of the above procedures with prompt written feedback to the contractor and identification of needed corrections and deadlines, with follow-up to determine the level of compliance; and
□ provision for supplying information obtained from the monitoring prior to scheduling rebidding and contract renewals so that this material can be used most effectively.

The same monitoring procedures apply to both publicly operated and contractor-operated facilities. States can then use the resulting information as a basis for comparisons of different types of facilities and thus obtain a better perspective on contractor performance.

10. *Evaluation.* From the state as well as local and national perspectives, systematic comprehensive evaluations of the costs and effectiveness of contracting secure correctional facilities are desirable. A state should require a comprehensive evaluation of contracting within three years of the contract award. When possible, the contracted facility should be compared to similar publicly operated facilities. On other than philosophical issues, debate over prison contracting is greatly enlightened by empirical findings. Failure to evaluate innovative experience is a great waste of resources.

11. *Community relations.* States establishing a new contracted facility or contracting for an existing one need a public relations plan. Good public relations are crucial for community education and acceptance. The state should fully inform community leaders and public correctional employees of any contracting deliberations. As early as possible, the media should be made aware of the contracting initiative. After a contract is awarded, the vendor should use community resources to operate the facility whenever appropriate, that is, hiring local people and buying supplies and services locally.

### Summary of Findings and Recommendations on Contracting for Limited Services in Correctional Facilities and for their Operation

The use of contracts is increasing, and the examples given illustrate different types of contracts as well as some of the problems experienced. Suggestions are offered on writing contracts to help ensure excellent performance.

The 1984 survey of contracting in correctional facilities asked the states about problems that they had encountered. The most common problem mentioned was monitoring performance, followed closely by poor service. Medical service contracts were popular because administrators believe providers offer better professional services and better staff than the state can.[43]

The states' experience in contracting for delivery of food services is mixed, but contracting appears to be a way of avoiding the problem of staffing what many perceive as jobs not appropriate for trained corrections officers. One state obtained better service by writing more detailed requirements into its RFPs.

States have not compared the quality and cost of contracting for educational services versus using state employees to teach. However, contracting states emphasize that contracting gives them added flexibility in offering different types of training to meet job market conditions. Additional experience is needed before meaningful judgments can be made about the relative success of different kinds of arrangements for food and educational services.

The history of contracting for management and operation of an entire state facility is short, but some lessons have already been learned. Spelling out in detail the contractor's responsibility regarding transportation, health, and library costs is needed, as are careful monitoring and evaluation of the contracting effort.

When considering whether to contract management of entire facilities, the states go through a process of careful analysis such as the one outlined above. The states should carefully monitor such aspects of prison administration as escape rates, prisoner health, contractor implementation of educational and other programs, and the number of complaints from prisoners and their families about any service. All these aspects of prison life should be compared with what is happening at similar state institutions. After a few years, the states should have a clearer picture of the advantages and disadvantages of contracting.

---

## ALTERNATIVES OTHER THAN CONTRACTING FOR USE OF THE PRIVATE SECTOR IN CORRECTIONAL ACTIVITIES

The other practical options for greater use of the private sector in correctional institutions are the use of volunteers, public-private partnerships, and donations.

## Volunteers in Corrections

Volunteers can be used as tutors in basic education, as vocational teachers, as recreational leaders, and as clerical workers. Volunteers frequently serve on advisory boards. Their use may be particularly appropriate for youth correctional facilities.

A policies and procedures document written by the Delaware Department of Correction summarizes how to build a useful band of volunteers for corrections facilities.[44] The procedures call for a statewide coordinator of volunteers in corrections and a coordinator at each institution to monitor all volunteers there. Volunteer applicants receive background checks and some psychological screening. Fraternization with prisoners is banned.

Goals are set by the volunteer and the supervisor to ensure growth in the job. The statewide coordinator receives a report on each volunteer after six months of "satisfactory" service. A second evaluation is made at the end of a year of service, and the volunteers then set goals for the next year. If volunteers are judged as failing to meet their goals, they are placed on probation for the coming year. Counselor advisors within the prison facilities also submit quarterly progress reports on their assigned volunteers.

The Delaware document seems to cover most of the problems that might occur with volunteer help. The use of volunteers in corrections obviously will vary from state to state and facility to facility, depending partly on the attitude of corrections administrators toward the value of help received versus the time and money spent in administration of a volunteer program.

## Public-Private Partnerships and Donations in Corrections

An example of public-private partnership in delivering services at correctional institutions is the frequent use of citizen-business people advisory boards, particularly for vocational education. These boards have three major purposes: they help the prison keep current with changes in technology and the employment market; they encourage donations of equipment, advice, and sometimes teaching talent from the community; and they can serve as conduits for employment of inmates when they are released.

The major donations are equipment for vocational education classes. Books are also donated to prison libraries, and money can be solicited for specific educational and cultural programs at correctional facilities.

Partnerships in prison industries are a major opportunity for states seeking ways to help inmates occupy their time "profitably." As mentioned at the beginning of this chapter, inmates are involved in industry programs in at least nine states. Two of the more creative programs are one at the Arizona Correctional Institution for Women, where inmates used computer terminals to make reservations for Best Western hotels, and an operation of a subsidiary of Control Data Corporation in Minnesota, whereby inmates manufactured disk drives and wire harnesses.[45]

The authors have not reviewed these programs in depth.[46]

## Summary of Findings and Recommendations on Alternatives to Contracting

Not enough is known about volunteer programs and the extent to which citizen advisory groups and donations are used by prison officials to judge whether these programs should be expanded. Public-private partnerships, especially to provide work experience for inmates, appear to be growing in popularity. The evidence suggests, however, that none of these opportunities is being followed to its potential. Citizens, businesses, and prison officials should probably work toward more use of the private sector in delivering these services.

### Notes

1. Camille K. Camp and George M. Camp, "Private Sector Involvement in Prison Services and Operations," prepared for the National Institute of Corrections, February 1985, p. 3.

2. Ibid., p. 6.

3. These data and most material in this section are taken from a survey done jointly by the Department of Corrections of the State of Delaware, The Urban Institute, and The Council of State Governments in the spring of 1987. For further information, see Delaware Department of Corrections, "Report on Service Alternatives for Food Services," 21 May 1987.

4. James A. Carroll, Food Services Coordinator, Florida Department of Corrections, telephone interview, March 1987,

5. Alan Shuman, Deputy Secretary, New Mexico Department of Corrections, telephone interview, April 1987.

6. Ibid.

7. Robert J. De Veau, Chief of Commissary and Food Services, Department of Corrections, Connecticut, telephone interview by The Urban Institute, March 1987.

8. David Lankford, Chief Dietician, Oklahoma Department of Corrections, telephone interview, 9 April 1987.

9. Ibid.

10. Camp and Camp, "Private Sector Involvement," Appendix E.

11. This section is based on a telephone interview by Urban Institute staff with David Carnahan, Director of Education, Washington Department of Corrections, December 1986, and materials received from him.

12. Washington Legislative Budget Committee, "Performance Audit: Prison Education and Training Programs," 19 August 1977.

13. Washington Department of Corrections, "Report to the Legislature: Academic and Vocational Training," 12 October 1981.

14. Maryland Department of Corrections, "Agreement with the Local Education Agency," August 1986.

15. Maryland Department of Education, "Agreement with the Local Education Agency, n.d.

16. The Urban Institute and The Council of State Governments, "A Process for Periodic Reviews of Alternative Ways to Deliver State Services," Working Group Papers for the State of Maryland, 1987.

17. Meetings of Urban Institute staff with Maryland corrections education officials, Fall 1986.

18. This section is based on telephone interviews with Roger Knudson, Coordinator of Correctional Education, Minnesota Department of Corrections, December 1986 and August 1987, and materials received from him.

19. Ibid.

20. Ibid.

21. Ibid.

22. Massachusetts Department of Youth Services, "A New Agenda: Education, Employment and Training, Substance Abuse Counseling," 1985 Annual Report.

23. The University of Texas at Austin, Lyndon B. Johnson School of Public Affairs, "Contracting Selected State Government Functions: Issues and Next Steps," 1986, p. 181.

24. W. J. Michael Cody and Andy D. Bennett, "The Privatization of Correctional Institutions: The Tennessee Experience," *Vanderbilt Law Review* (May 1987), p. 847.

25. Ibid.

26. *The Privatization Review* (Summer 1986), p. 60; Georgina Fiordalisi, "Lease Deal Finances New Missouri Prison," *City and State* (August 1986); and Harms and Allen, op. cit.

27. Judith Hackett, et al., Issues in Contracting for the Private Operation of Prisons and Jails (Washington, D.C.: National Institute of Justice, 1987). We discuss here several local facilities because some of their experience will be useful to state authorities.

28. Information on Texas prisons is taken from "Companies Selected to Operate 2 Prisons," *Austin American-Statesman*, 20 October 1987, p. B2.

29. Bay County, Florida, "Bay County Detention Facilities Contract between Corrections Corporation of America and Bay County, Florida, September 3, 1985," p. 37.

30. Hamilton County, Tennessee, "Hamilton County Correction Facilities Agreement," 1984, pp. 6 and 10.

31. Bay County contract, Appendix B, p. 22; and "Hamilton County Agreement," Appendix A, pp. 14–15.

32. Kentucky, "Request for Proposals for 200-Inmate Correctional Facility," 12 April 1985, p. 30–7.

33. This section is based on interviews by staff of The Urban Institute and The Council of State Governments with Kentucky corrections officials and the contractor in Frankfort and Marion, Kentucky, May 1986, and on Kentucky's "Request for Proposals."

34. Kentucky, "Request for Proposals," p. 40–2.

35. Ibid., p. 30–10.

36. Ibid., p. 30–11.

37. U.S. Corrections Corporation, proposal papers, July–November 1985.

38. Urban Institute telephone interviews with Marion Adjustment Center officials, July 1986 and December 1987.

39. Ibid.

40. Ibid.

41. This section is based primarily on "Issues in Contracting for Prisons."

42. Charles H. Logan, "Proprietary Prisons," in Lynne Goodstein and Doris L. Mac-Kenzie, eds., The American Prison: Issues in Research and Policy (New York: Plenum, 1988), p. 18.

43. Ibid., p. 11.

44. Delaware Department of Correction, "Policies and Procedures: Volunteers," December 1986.

45. Kenneth J. Harms and W. Frank Allen, "Privatizing Prisons," American City and County (August 1987), pp. 30–31.

46. Some of these efforts are described in Keon S. Chi, "The Private Sector in State Correctional Industries: The Control Data Program in Minnesota," Innovations, The Council of State Governments, August 1985.

# Chapter Three

# USE OF THE PRIVATE SECTOR FOR SERVICE DELIVERY IN STATE PARKS AND RECREATION AREAS

*Joan W. Allen*

Public use of state parks and recreation areas is increasing. At the same time, state funds are shrinking. State park budgets declined 17 percent in real dollars between 1981 and 1984. How can administrators continue present services using less financial resources?[1] Officials across the United States are looking for ways.

Services performed in state park and recreation areas include:

□ road and grounds maintenance,
□ custodial and garbage services,
□ provision of lifeguards at beaches and pools,
□ rental of campground space and boats,
□ issuance of fishing and hunting licenses,
□ selling of food and other sundries,
□ rental of cabin space, and
□ nature education programs.

Some alternative ways of delivering state services are already in common use. States traditionally *contract* for major construction in parks, and they frequently *franchise* private firms for food sales, boat rental and other services. Concessions are a hybrid approach, combining features of both contracts and franchises. A formal contract exists between the state and the contractor, but the contractor obtains at least a substantial portion of its revenues directly from the public.

Parks directors recently began taking advantage of further variations in service delivery. They are using *volunteers* more. They are soliciting *donations* of private land. *Public-private partnerships* are being formed to raise money, acquire land, and manage it. Another variation is the use of Youth Conservation Corps members. They are paid minimum wages for work usually done by state employees who must earn higher wages but for whom positions cannot be funded.

Park officials are also involving the public more than ever before in planning for parks and recreation areas, both to save planning money and to increase the public's interest in lobbying governments for park funds.

This chapter covers the principal ways in which park and recreation officials are using contracting, franchising, voluntarism, public-private partnerships, and donations from the private sector.

## CONTRACTS AND CONCESSIONS

Until the last eight years or so, when the use of volunteers increased markedly, contracting with private vendors for delivery of some services was the major way state parks tried to cut costs while maintaining quality services.

In Massachusetts, for example, the Division of Forests and Parks of the Department of Environmental Management contracts with the nonprofit Massachusetts Audubon Society to provide staff in the Boston Harbor Island State Park. The society hires managers and interns who enforce rules and provide other administrative, programming, and educational services at one-third the in-house cost, according to The Conservation Foundation.[2]

The Pennsylvania Bureau of State Parks negotiates contracts with nonprofit groups for the operation and maintenance of historical structures. One private group raises its own funds for rehabilitation and restoration work.[3]

The Missouri State Parks system contracts with a local motorcycle club for the operation and maintenance of some multiple use areas requiring extensive upkeep.[4]

For detailed examples of contracting (including concessions) for state parks services, the authors interviewed park administrators and reviewed relevant documents from Delaware, Florida, South Carolina, and Virginia. We also talked with a Wisconsin park official about operation of some state parks by private organizations.

### Delaware Contracts[5]

#### DESCRIPTION

Until 1986, Delaware contracted for few park services except construction. It began with relatively small contracts, partly because it needed additional custodial services at seashore rest rooms, serving an increasing number of participants. With increased amounts of trash in the parks, the state contracted for trash removal from dumpsters.

The state also contracts for boat captain service from Delaware City to Ft. Delaware State Park, for repair of office machines, and for Jiffy-Lube service for central office vehicles at Dover. Uniforms for both seasonal and full-time personnel are now supplied and laundered by a contractor.

Contracts under $5,000 are not bid competitively. For contracts of $5,000–10,000 the state must contact five potential bidders. For contracts of more than $10,000, the state advertises its requests for proposals (RFPs). Contracting (for other than construction) comprises only about 1 percent of the Park Division's budget.

### Delaware Concessions

*DESCRIPTION*

At one time, state employees provided food and other services in state parks. To shed direct responsibility, the parks division franchised 16 services to for-profit organizations.

The bidding process typically results in a three-year contract with a two-year renewal option. The state parks director sees the need for longer contracts in some cases to encourage the private sector to make needed capital improvements (e.g., to a marina).

Contract awards are based on an assessment of potential quality of the service and profits to the state. For most concession contracts, the state receives 20 percent or less of the gross receipts. Small concessionaires have had serious financial difficulties with this arrangement. Future concession contracts will be negotiated for a flat fee paid to the state plus a smaller percentage to lessen the concessionaire's financial risk.

All food services are delivered through concessions. Other concessions include boat repair and charter, bait and tackle, fish cleaning, boarding of horses and riding lessons, and tennis lessons.

*ASSESSMENT*

Contract and concession performance and cost have not been formally evaluated. Informal oral evaluations are used instead. Contractors and concessionaires were generally rated satisfactory by parks officials. They indicated that the lack of sufficient state personnel and the difficulty of hiring additional employees necessitate the use of contracting and concessions.

## Florida Contracts

### DESCRIPTION[6]

The major contracts for services in Florida state parks and recreation areas, other than construction, are for garbage collection and linen service at rental cabins. The contracts range from approximately $2,400 to $12,000 for garbage collection and from $3,000 to $12,000 for linen service. The state also contracts on an ad hoc basis for some other services, including an unusual contract for $102,000 with the University of Florida for research on the exact route of the DeSoto Trail.

Garbage collection contracts were first issued in 1978, when the state raised landfill charges. Most parks are served by the same contractors franchised by nearby localities for garbage collection in their communities. The contracts are usually for one or two years, with one- or two-year renewal clauses. Contracting is competitive when a contract exceeds $3,000. Two to four vendors usually bid for the fixed price contracts.

### ASSESSMENT

When a contract exceeds $3,000, a quarterly report on performance must be filed by the Parks Division with the Department of General Services. This report only notes whether performance is satisfactory or unsatisfactory, with a brief discussion.[7]

The state has not done a detailed cost analysis of contracting but is confident that it is saving money by freeing park rangers and equipment for duties other than garbage collection. State landfill fees paid when park employees were handling garbage have at least tripled in the last 10 years.

The state has not been pleased with its linen service at public rental cabins. In some locations, only one bid was made for the service. Delivery is occasionally late or nonexistent. But billing is the major problem, and linen service companies sometimes double-bill. The state suggested to park managers that they keep written records of linens delivered to help alleviate this problem. A state official judged linen service performance "just below satisfactory."[8]

**Florida Concessions[9]**

*DESCRIPTION*

Private for-profit concessionaires operate food services, canoe rentals, and ferryboat and tour services. The Coral Reef Park Company employs 50–75 people, depending upon the season, at an "underwater" state park in the Keys formerly owned by the federal government. In contrast, the park has 20–25 full-time state employees. Until several years ago, state employees were responsible for some of the services now provided by private companies. The state had increasing difficulty hiring and retaining qualified staff.

The lack of legislative authorization for what parks officials considered sufficient funding and staffing and the relative ease of administering private sector activities contributed to an expansion of concessions by parks officials. Some state officials are also interested in expanding concessions to increase revenues for park operation. Some officials think that copying the federal practice of granting long-term leases (10–20 years) to major concessionaires would improve services. Such leases would favor the concessionaires by yielding lower profits to the state but could ensure better quality than shorter-term agreements.

Florida law does not require competitive bidding for concessions, but the state usually has no trouble securing several bids on concessions in urban parks. In rural areas, there is sometimes only one bidder. All concessions in Florida are currently run by for-profit organizations.

Concessionaires complain about the percentage of gross profits that goes to the state. The state tried administering franchises whereby the concessionaires paid fixed fees, but it has since returned to percentage contracts due to concessionaire complaints about the fixed fee system. Under the fixed fee system, state profits ranged from 23 percent to about 40 percent of gross profits, too high a percentage for most concessionaires to prosper. The result is that some concessionaires, those renting canoes for example, have cut maintenance, resulting in poorer service to the public. Because of the difficulty in finding a concessionaire, state employees run a small store at Stephen Foster State Park that grosses only $4,000-$5,000 per month.

A senior state parks official pays a surprise visit to each concessionaire at least once a year. The park supervisor fills out quarterly concessionaire evaluation forms at each park and sends them to state park headquarters. The four-page form includes financial information and findings of the park supervisor—for example, on whether stock items are appropriate for the park, prices are fair and comparable with others in the general area, and employees are courteous at all times.

## ASSESSMENT

Florida state parks officials are generally pleased with their concessionaires, and the central parks office plans to expand the use of concessions in the next few years. The state office will also study whether to allow concessionaires to charge higher fees at the same time that the state reduces admission and other fees. The intent is to support the parks financially by charging fees more in line with the cost of services provided to park users. But officials remain divided on whether the main function of concessions is to produce revenues or to provide a continuing predictable service. That service is assured by the state's giving concessionaires rights for longer periods (such as 10 years) and allowing them to keep a higher percentage of profits.

### South Carolina Contracts and Concessions[10]

## DESCRIPTION

The State of South Carolina contracts for three services in its parks: mechanical equipment servicing, security guards as needed during the summer, and garbage pickup. For years the state has contracted for some mechanical servicing. It began contracting for garbage collection in about 1974 and for security guards in about 1978.

Approximately 20 percent of mechanical equipment servicing in the parks is on contract. The largest state contract, for about $16,000 annually, is for servicing mechanical equipment at one of its larger parks. All security guards are employed under contract, and 90 percent of garbage pickup is contracted for (wherever contractors can be located). The largest security guard contract is for about $3,000 and the largest garbage pickup contract is for about $3,600.

Cost is the major reason for the state contracts. Contracting for garbage service saves approximately two-thirds of the total cost because the state makes no capital investment in trucks. Security guards are hired for seasonal work when it is difficult to get state employees. Contracting for complicated mechanical equipment servicing is cheaper when park employees do not have the necessary technical knowledge.

South Carolina uses a bidding process for all contracts and generally receives four or five bids on all services. Contracts usually run for one year; all are fixed-priced contracts. Mechanical services and security guards are rebid after each contract. Garbage collection contracts have automatic renewal clauses with provision for annual price increases.

The contracts contain no performance incentives, but they have performance requirements. Park superintendents monitor performance. When performance is poor, the superintendent sends both the vendor and a higher state parks official a complaint form. If performance does not improve, the contract is canceled or is simply not renewed.

During the 1970s and early 1980s, the state leased the management of two restaurants and several riding stables, receiving a percentage of gross profits. But the state took over the services in 1982 after numerous complaints about sanitation, quality of products, and personnel. South Carolina has no plans for future leasing of concessions; part-time employees, mostly college students, now deliver these services.

*ASSESSMENT*

The state parks procurement officer stated that contractor performance in all three areas of service was satisfactory. South Carolina plans to continue contracting for these services. No formal evaluations have been conducted of the quality and cost of contracting compared with service by public employees. One garbage contract was canceled recently; however, the state has had fewer complaints about garbage collection since the service was contracted for.

The state is trying to develop additional contract bidders to keep quality up and costs down, particularly for garbage pickup. What they do is to call Chambers of Commerce and landfill operators, some of whom are listed in the yellow pages of phone directories.

**Virginia Contracts and Concessions[11]**

*DESCRIPTION*

Refuse collection and linen service for rental cabins account for virtually all parks service contracts in Virginia. Sometimes the state contracts with county governments for refuse collection.

The major use of private firms in Virginia parks is for operating *concessions*—food service, swimming area supervision, bicycle and horse rentals, and camp stores. State employees supervise all camping and cabin rental. Concessions account for 25–40 percent of park personnel during the summer, particularly in parks with many labor-intensive jobs.

The state has used concessions since it opened the state parks system in 1936 because of the lower cost of private sector labor and the costly red tape of state purchasing processes. The concessionaires are usually local business owners who operate the facilities part-time to complement their year-round businesses. All concessionaires are for-profit organizations, but the state is investigating the possibility of a nonprofit group's running a small souvenir shop in a rural area; no for-profit entrepreneur is interested.

The major difficulty with concessions is finding enough bidders. In the past, many concessions were operated by families more willing than larger organizations to work longer hours for smaller profits. These families are hard to replace. Because of low business volume at some concessions, there were no bidders, so state employees operate the services.

The cost of liability insurance is a significant problem for small businesses that might run concessions with a limited trade volume.

The concessionaires file both monthly and annual reports. Income reports are required monthly. The annual reports include information on gross income, labor costs as a percentage of income, merchandise costs, utilities, and maintenance costs, liability insurance costs, and the fee paid to the state. Two appraisals of inventory are required: one by the concessionaire and one by a disinterested appraiser.

Individual park superintendents monitor the concessions daily. They prepare park inspection reports in which the inspector rates performance in each part of the park, including concessions.

ASSESSMENT

Overall, parks officials believe that concessions are running satisfactorily. In 1986 the Division of Parks and Recreation made a study to determine whether some concessions could be operated more economically or more profitably if they were run by state employees.

The state conducted a staffing and merchandise requirement analysis of each park and estimated the wages for state employees to replace concessionaire employees. It also estimated what the state purchasing process might add to the price of goods purchased concessionaires. The amount of sales tax paid by concessionaires was also considered.

The state conducted a staffing and merchandise requirement analysis of each park and estimated the wages for state employees to replace concessionaire employees. It also estimated what the state purchasing process might add to the price of goods purchased by concessionaires. The amount of sales tax paid by concessionaires was also considered.

The study concluded that "the profit now experienced by the concessionaires would be offset by the additional personnel costs and purchasing requirements and that concession operations run by the State would operate at a loss."[12] The report recommended that concessionaires receive a higher percentage of the fees charged in some cases to "offset insurance costs" to the provider.[13] The study found that "a concession grossing $35,000 for the season is a break-even situation" for the entrepreneur.[14]

### Wisconsin Agreements on Operations of Small Parks[15]

*DESCRIPTION*

In passing the budget for the 1981–83 fiscal biennium in the State of Wisconsin, the legislature reduced funds for the Bureau of Parks and Recreation in the Department of Natural Resources. The parks bureau was faced with the alternatives of either closing 13 small properties (each about 200 acres or less) or having them operated at greatly reduced funding by local townships, counties, or private nonprofit organizations such as Lions Clubs. Major maintenance remained the responsibility of the state.

The state was paying an average of about $18,000 a year, including major maintenance, to operate each park, with no permanent full-time state employees involved. It paid the local governmental and private organizations $2,000 annually for operation of each park, using some state equipment. Agreements were for terms of one, two, or three years. Volunteers did most of the work. (The state has not recruited much volunteer help for the parks.) The organizations operate the parks on entrance and/or camping fees and have had no trouble "making ends meet."

One agreement, begun in 1981, was with the Solon Springs Civic Club for the operation and maintenance of Lucius Woods State

Park.[16] The two-year agreement called for the club to mow grass and lawn areas, clean up litter and solid waste, clean the rest rooms, operate and maintain the beach, and provide police and fire protection in the park. Major maintenance remained the responsibility of the state. Short-term maintenance, such as painting, glass or screen repair, minor roof leaks, maintenance of pumps and water systems, and repair of minor vandalism was the responsibility of the club.[17]

The state paid the club $2,500 annually to help offset costs. The club was authorized to collect a user fee from park visitors to further offset its expenses.[18]

### ASSESSMENT

When the 1983–85 budget increased funding for the parks, the state took several of them back. It was not dissatisfied with the local organizations but felt that it should operate the parks when it had the money.

The state parks bureau is trying to divest itself of several small parks, turning them into local parks that would be the responsibility of local governments, which may be able to operate the parks with less money than it costs the state.

### Summary of Findings and Recommendations on Contracts and Concessions in State Parks

Except for construction, large states generally make limited use of contracts for park services. Contracts seem to comprise only a small proportion of total park budgets when construction contracts are excluded. Contracting is sometimes used for linen services and other small maintenance activities.

Some states have had difficulty finding enough firms to bid on small contracts, particularly in rural areas.

The use of a hybrid of contracting and franchising—concessions—is popular, particularly for food and housing services. Concessions are fairly common for food and accommodations services, stores, rentals of sports equipment such as bicycles, boats and fishing tackle, and horseback riding and tennis.

State officials interviewed for this study and the literature on state contracting for park services indicate that contracts and concessions are not closely monitored (except for costs) and that states perceive a need for closer monitoring. Some states have used ratings to monitor concessionaire performance, but we were unable to identify any significant formal rating processes. Most contractor evaluations are informal visual inspections by park supervisors.

The State of Virginia evaluated its concessions practices and costs to see whether it should switch back to state employee operation. The study was primarily a financial analysis, not an evaluation of service quality. Here the state found that it would likely operate at a loss if it switched back to state operation.

Although information is limited on the cost-effectiveness of contracts and concessions, the following recommendations may be useful:

1. The states should review the services at each park every year or two to determine whether the current mode of operation (contracting, concessions, or state employee operation) needs to be revised. Changes should be considered for facilities with either financial or service quality problems.
2. State parks and recreation agencies should institute more formal quality control procedures, including systematic inspections by trained observers and client feedback instruments. Samples of clients could be interviewed as they check out of facilities or leave the park. The results could be used both as feedback to current providers and as an aid in determining whether changes in operation are needed.
3. Contracts and concession agreements should contain explicit performance standards for service quality—preferably with rewards and penalties for exceeding or failing to meet the standards. (Performance standards and monitoring could also be applied to the operation of facilities by state employees.)
4. The state should consider encouraging constructive competition between state employees and the private sector, permitting both to bid on the operation of certain services every few years. This option is fairly radical, one likely to meet considerable opposition. It might be useful to see whether the resulting competition can reduce costs and improve service quality. These competitions should be based on quality as well as price. The winning bidder should be monitored carefully to ensure that citizens receive the quality of service that they were promised.

## VOLUNTEERS

Most states find it difficult to acquire funds for assigning staff to educational work. Thirty state park directors (60 percent of the 50 states) reported in 1985 that they were making significantly more use of volunteers and nonprofit groups to provide visitor services.[19] They are using volunteers in a variety of ways. For example, in a campground host program in Kansas, in exchange for free recreational vehicle camping privileges and nominal wages, participants greet visitors, provide information, collect overnight fees, and perform minor maintenance tasks. At Hither Hills State Park, on Long Island, the Camper Assistance Program involves volunteers in visitor programs in exchange for extended vacation time.[20]

### Some Examples

Several states have statewide volunteer organizations, such as Outdoor Washington and Volunteers for Outdoor Colorado (VOC). Reacting to government budget cuts and the increased recreational use of public lands, VOC was organized in 1984 to preserve and improve such areas. It solicits ideas from members, government agencies, and users. After setting priorities, it seeks funding from both government and private sources. Then VOC crew leaders and volunteers do the work. Projects include tree and shrub planting, trail and shelter construction and maintenance, erosion control and steambed improvements. More than 2,000 volunteers had completed 17 projects worth nearly $200,000 by the end of the 1986 season.[21]

Some state parks have organized "friends" groups that do historic research, fund raising, and lobbying. Oregon permits private associations to generate funds for interpretive services through sales in parks. The services are provided in the park where the funds were raised.[22]

A volunteer organization called Tahoe Rim Trail (TRT) has a most ambitious project. TRT combines the efforts of volunteers from organizations ranging from adult horseback riding clubs to the Girl Scouts. The group is advised by the U.S. Forest Service and the administrator of Nevada's state parks.[23] TRT is supervising the construction by volunteers of a 150-mile trail around Lake Tahoe, located in both California and Nevada. Much of the money to build the trail is donated by foundations and professional organizations such as Soroptimist International.[24]

Adopt-a-Trail and Adopt-a-Park programs are prevalent throughout the country. Individual citizens and groups maintain portions of public trails and work in state parks.

Volunteers can often save the states much money. For example, the La Junta Trail near Taos, New Mexico, was closed because it seriously needed repair. Bids ranged from $85,000 to $105,000. Volunteers for the Outdoors (VFO), a private state group, completed the project for $22,000—$3,000 for VFO administrative expenses and $19,000 for materials.[25]

A few years ago, Michigan assessed the worth of its recreation volunteers at more than $10 million.[26] Parks officials believe that the benefits of volunteers may go beyond the work they do. Officials comment:

Volunteers also offer staff new insight into problem situations. Volunteers on task forces or on ad hoc committees provide a fresh perspective and energy that can sometimes stimulate staff who have become mired in routine activity. . . . Volunteers can also provide staff a needed respite from operational concerns and enable them to use their creative energies in a productive fashion.[27]

Unions sometimes oppose volunteer programs. One way to enlist their support is to involve their members in woodworking, electrical classes, and other special projects or as club advisors.[28]

A special hybrid is agreements between governments and nonprofit organizations whereby the latter receive some money for their efforts in parks, particularly in planning and interpretation, but at a lower cost than what it would take for the state to do the work with public employees. In a pilot program in Massachusetts, the state cooperated with four nonprofit organizations for an interpretive program at Robinson State Park, a management plan for Halibut Point State Park, and planning a state trails network.[29]

A researcher concluded, after extensive interviews with government and nonprofit participants in the programs, that such agreements are likely to be advantageous to state parks directors, but he added some caveats about selecting the nonprofit:[30]

1. Make sure that the central mission of the nonprofit closely matches the state's objectives of the project.
2. The methods normally used by an organization should also closely match the approaches to be employed in the project.
3. The "normal operating area" of the nonprofit should include the region to be served by the project. Geographic range is particularly important with nonprofits because they tend to operate in localized, fairly parochial territories.
4. A nonprofit organization involved in a cooperative agreement should be fairly stable in terms of staff, objectives, and finances.

5. Because nonprofits tend to have crowded agendas, the person in charge of the cooperative project should be committed to the effort, responsible, and a "mover."
6. If volunteers are needed for a successful project, check to be sure the group is oriented toward using volunteers, not just paid staff.
7. The nonprofit chosen should either have the inhouse expertise to perform the required tasks or know explicitly where to find the capability.
8. Lobbying organizations are generally inappropriate contractors because their involvement in a cause may create too many conflict of interest problems with a government.
9. Look for a nonprofit that offers potential for long-term nonproject-related benefits.

The following information about volunteer programs is for the same states whose officials were interviewed about contracting for park services: Delaware, Florida, South Carolina, and Virginia. The discussion is based on those interviews and the materials provided by the states.

**Delaware**

*DESCRIPTION*

A Campground Host Program was begun in Delaware parks in the summer of 1987. As in the Kansas program mentioned earlier, Delaware gives experienced campers free rental of campsites at state parks and recreation areas in return for their welcoming other campers, sometimes collecting fees when campers arrive "after hours," checking rest rooms, and generally helping campers with problems. This exchange eliminates the need for additional state rangers or attendants. State employees were not displaced—the parks had been understaffed.

For several years, volunteers in Delaware parks have assisted state naturalists in giving talks. Other volunteers collect fees and paint buildings. The Boy Scouts, Girl Scouts, and other service agencies help with grounds maintenance. Volunteers worked a total of 1,290 hours from May through September of 1986, worth an estimated $6,900.[32]

"Contracts" are written with some volunteers, guaranteeing a certain amount and quality of work. The state is increasing use of these contracts because some state employees complain that volunteers are not always reliable or helpful.

## ASSESSMENT

State parks officials are generally pleased with the volunteers, and the central park office is encouraging increased use of volunteers because of a hiring freeze on state employees. Volunteers currently represent a savings of approximately 1 percent of the state parks budget. Contracting with volunteers is designed to improve volunteer performance.

## Florida[33]

### DESCRIPTION

Florida uses volunteers for two distinct purposes: routine maintenance, special litter clean ups, and light construction work (e.g., fence building) and professional-level studies (e.g., on resource management). The less skilled duties are performed mainly by crews from the Sierra Club, Boy Scouts, Audubon Society, Pioneers of America and other organizations. Because of its high percentage of retirees, Florida has an advantage in recruiting qualified volunteers.

The Florida Department of Natural Resources expects to have a statewide recruiter for volunteers in its parks soon. This state employee will contact service organizations and private companies throughout the state to sell the idea of citizens' volunteering for work in state parks. If this effort proves successful, the department may hire regional recruiters as well.

Volunteers have worked in Florida state parks for more than 10 years. They have not supplanted state employees but instead have augmented their work. Volunteers are monitored by individual park managers. For calendar year 1986, Florida parks reported a total of 30,000 hours of volunteer time,[34] the equivalent of about 19 full-time personnel. These figures are for individual volunteers only and do not include volunteer help from private groups.

Florida's Division of Recreation and Parks has a formal volunteer services policy.[35] It requires volunteer application forms, a volunteer agreement form (signed by the volunteer and a park official), a semiannual report of all volunteer hours during the previous six months, and a certificate of appreciation for each volunteer. The policy manual stipulates "control" to ensure that services are provided satisfactorily, but it does not require formal evaluations of volunteers' work.

### ASSESSMENT

The state has not evaluated the quality of volunteer work or estimated the amount of money that volunteers save. The official in charge of the volunteer program judges overall performance "very satisfactory." He knows of no particular problems that have surfaced and believes that the state's special effort to gain press coverage of volunteer activities has contributed to the success of the program.

### South Carolina[36]

### DESCRIPTION

The legislature formally authorized the use of volunteers in South Carolina parks in 1978. Approximately 1.5 percent of the work in the state parks is done by volunteers: 13,198 hours in 1986, the equivalent of about eight full-time personnel.

South Carolina began using volunteers to save personnel costs and also to enhance citizen support for parks. Volunteers have not replaced any state employees but instead have augmented their work. Recently, the state initiated sessions to train supervisors in the best methods of using volunteers. The state plans to expand its use of volunteers.

Following the lead of other states, South Carolina initiated a Campground Host Program in 1987, intending to expand it in 1988. The hosts provide information and assistance to campers and in return receive free campsites. Exhibit 3.1 describes the program and lists "do's and don't's" for the volunteers. The Campground Host Program is used in many parks across the country.[37]

The most sophisticated parks and recreation volunteer program in the state, at Charles Towne Landing State Park, is supervised by a full-time state employee. The supervisor was a volunteer before being hired as assistant supervisor by the state.

At Charles Towne and some other state parks, volunteers punch time clocks. Volunteers at Charles Towne engage in a greater variety of work than at most other state parks: grounds maintenance; interpretive programs on a sailing ship, in a museum, and at other

Exhibit 3.1  CAMPGROUND HOST PROGRAM

The Park Division will utilize volunteers to implement a Campground Host program at selected parks. This program will be a part of the Volunteers in the Parks program and be administered in accordance with the established procedures. The Park Superintendent will serve as the sponsor for their "host." District Superintendents will serve as the coordinator for this program in their respective districts.

District Superintendents will select parks to be involved in the "Host" program. Park Superintendents, serving as the sponsor, will develop and convey job descriptions and requirements. As a minimum, the requirement will include the following:

1. *Major objectives of the job:* To serve as a Park Division representative to campers and other park visitors by providing assistance and serving as an information source; assist the park in providing a quality campground operation.

2. *Major responsibilities:* To be available to campers in order to render assistance and provide information; to ensure that the facilities and grounds are maintained in a condition that will ensure camper satisfaction.

3. *Type of work performed:* Provide information to campers and other visitors about the park, its operation and the surrounding area. Provide general assistance to campers. Monitor problems and obtain assistance from park staff. Check facilities for maintenance problems and provide staff with information concerning the problems. Be the primary contact point between staff and campers. Work in program activities, if qualified. Perform light housekeeping activities on grounds and facilities.

4. *Time commitment and duration of program:* The host will provide a minimum of four hours per day, five days a week, actively pursuing the items covered in "Type of work performed." In addition, the hosts must be available to provide assistance on an as needed basis at any time they are in the park.

   The "Host" program will begin on a date no earlier than the first of March, as determined by the sponsor, and will terminate no later than the first of November. The host must agree not to be absent from the campground for more than one week during the program period, or the host will be terminated.

5. *Type of supervision:* The sponsor (Park Superintendent) will be the primary supervisor. In the Superintendent's absence, the next level of personnel will assume the supervision.

6. *Qualifications required:* The host must be in a physical condition that will allow the items covered under "Type of work performed." The host must be able to deal tactfully and cordially with the public.

7. *Sponsor:* Park Superintendent.

An agreement must be prepared for each host (or hostess) per example in the Volunteer in the Parks Program information.

Additional information is attached that is pertinent to implementations of this program.

Exhibit 3.1 *Continued*

*DETAILS OF HOST JOB*
I. Duties:
  A. Do's:
    1. Pick up trash around campsites when site is unoccupied.
    2. Rake sites when site is unoccupied.
    3. Do touchup work on restrooms.
    4. Make list of maintenance needs.
    5. Know personnel on duty and how to contact them.
    6. Know phone numbers of personnel housed in park.
    7. Give information on:
      a. park facilities and related fees
      b. local points of interest
      c. nearby parks
      d. nearby stores
      e. nearby medical assistance
      f. park activities and programs.
    8. May work in area of programs if qualified.
    9. Should inform campers or visitors when they are in violation of rules or regulations.
  B. Don't's:
    1. Do not operate any type of motorized equipment.
    2. Do not handle park funds in any way.
    3. Do not take any action beyond an information level when violations are noticed—contact duty ranger to handle these situations.
II. Use of Campground:
  A. Site will be designated near campground entrance and signed as "Campground Host." Utilities will be provided at no cost.
  B. Requirement for moving every 14 days will not be in effect for this individual.
  C. No permanent or semi-permanent facilities can be constructed on this site. The site will not give the appearance of a year-round resident.
III. Criteria for Program:
  A. Position will be posted in park facilities as to availability.
  B. Individual may be single or married.
  C. Must not have other employment during the volunteer period.
  D. Term of program is to be established by the sponsor in accordance with other directives. Agreement may be terminated by either party. Insufficient or unsatisfactory work will be grounds for termination. Absence from the park for more than one week may result in termination of the agreement.
  E. Hours of work to be set up with the Superintendent, for five days per week and four hours per day. Total hours per week—twenty hours.
  F. Insurance:
    1. Workmen's Compensation not available.
    2. Insurance for job-related accidents covered in volunteer program information.
IV. Uniforms and Appearance:
  A. Shirts and name tags to be provided.
  B. Hosts' appearance must reflect a positive image to the visitor.

Source: South Carolina Parks Division, 1987.

sites in the park; research and graphics; and some food service. Charles Towne is outside Charleston, a major city that supplies a large pool of volunteers. Volunteers are recruited through the newspaper and by staff visits to senior citizen groups, garden clubs, youth groups, including the Scouts, and other organizations.

### ASSESSMENT

State park officials generally rate volunteer work in the parks as satisfactory, with work at Charles Towne Landing "very satisfactory." The park department plans to expand the use of volunteers.

Charles Towne Landing has experienced some problems. In the summer, parents sometimes drop their children off, ostensibly for them to do volunteer work. This practice sometimes results in the park's acting as babysitter for children 10–16 years old. Another problem is a small number of volunteers who punch the time clock and then disappear until time to punch out, particularly on weekends, when the acting coordinator is not on duty.

Volunteers are evaluated at Charles Towne after their first six months and then annually. Poor workers are not encouraged to continue. Evaluation procedures are not uniform throughout the parks.

### Virginia[38]

### DESCRIPTION

In Virginia, volunteers at state parks help maintain roads and trails, staff visitor centers, provide interpretive services, do general office and clerical work, and are occasional guest speakers. Citizens, along with state and federal representatives, serve on an advisory committee for a new park, New River, being developed along an abandoned railroad right-of-way.

At Seashore and Smith Mountain Lake, volunteers provide about 5–8 percent of the services. They completely operate the Visitors Centers in these two parks. The Friends of Smith Mountain Lake distributes funds donated by a local citizen.

Virginia supervisors rate each volunteer using the assessment form shown in exhibit 3.2. Although the state asks for monthly ratings, volunteers are usually rated only at the end of their summer service. The ratings are used principally as references if a citizen wants to volunteer during a successive season.

Volunteers' routine benefits consist of free cabin and campsite

Exhibit 3.2  VOLUNTEER ASSESSMENT IN VIRGINIA STATE PARKS

Name of Volunteer _____    Position _____

Supervisor _____    Date _____

Date of last evaluation _____

Use the following scale:

| 1 - 2 - 3 | 4 - 5 - 6 | 7 - 8 - 9 |
|-----------|-----------|-----------|
| Excellent | Good | Poor |

Staff: Please rate the volunteer in each of these areas:

1) Works to Capacity                1 - 2 - 3 - 4 - 5 - 6 - 7 - 8 - 9
2) Demonstrates                     1 - 2 - 3 - 4 - 5 - 6 - 7 - 8 - 9
   Resourcefulness
3) Demonstrates                     1 - 2 - 3 - 4 - 5 - 6 - 7 - 8 - 9
   Enthusiasm
4) Demonstates                      1 - 2 - 3 - 4 - 5 - 6 - 7 - 8 - 9
   Responsibility
5) Demonstates                      1 - 2 - 3 - 4 - 5 - 6 - 7 - 8 - 9
   Dependability
6) Accepts Supervision              1 - 2 - 3 - 4 - 5 - 6 - 7 - 8 - 9
7) Gets Along with Other            1 - 2 - 3 - 4 - 5 - 6 - 7 - 8 - 9
   Staff
8) Gets Along with                  1 - 2 - 3 - 4 - 5 - 6 - 7 - 8 - 9
   Clients
9) Gets Along with Other            1 - 2 - 3 - 4 - 5 - 6 - 7 - 8 - 9
   Volunteers
COMMENTS: _____

_____

_____

VOLUNTEER: Please rate your job and the staff in each of these areas:

1) Staff Support                    1 - 2 - 3 - 4 - 5 - 6 - 7 - 8 - 9
2) Staff Supervision                1 - 2 - 3 - 4 - 5 - 6 - 7 - 8 - 9
3) Working Climate                  1 - 2 - 3 - 4 - 5 - 6 - 7 - 8 - 9
4) Training Received                1 - 2 - 3 - 4 - 5 - 6 - 7 - 8 - 9
5) Job Assignment                   1 - 2 - 3 - 4 - 5 - 6 - 7 - 8 - 9
6) Staff Attitude                   1 - 2 - 3 - 4 - 5 - 6 - 7 - 8 - 9
COMMENTS: _____

_____

_____

Source: Virginia Division of Parks and Recreation.

privileges or seasonal or permanent park passes. The lifetime pass is awarded when a volunteer accrues 300 hours in one calendar year. Exhibit 3.3 shows Virginia's schedule of benefits for volunteers.

Volunteers have not replaced any state employees, but they have been used for new projects for which employees might have been hired. State employees have not objected to this practice.

The Virginia Department of Volunteerism periodically holds workshops to train particular department officials in their recruitment and use of volunteers.

Exhibit 3.3  BENEFITS AND A TIME/BENEFIT RECORD SHEET FOR VOLUNTEERS IN VIRGINIA STATE PARKS

| Benefit | Initial service | 16 hrs. | 32 hrs. | 64 hrs. | 100 hrs. | 300 hrs. |
|---|---|---|---|---|---|---|
| Pot luck supper | X | | | | | |
| Volunteer ID badge | X | | | | | |
| Superintendent's certificate of appreciation | | X | | | | |
| One year pass to the park of service | | | X | | | |
| One year pass to all Virginia state parks | | | | X | | |
| Personalized name tag | | | | X | | |
| Commissioner's certificate of appreciation | | | | | X | |
| Cabin privileges (7 nights maximum) | | | | | X | |
| Campsite privileges (14 nights maximum) | | | | | X | |
| Lifetime pass to all Virginia state parks | | | | | | X |

(All hours must be accrued within one year's time)

Source: Virginia Division of Parks and Recreation,

ASSESSMENT

The negative attitude of some park directors and other state employees toward volunteers inhibits increased use of volunteers. A park official rated volunteer work satisfactorily overall but stated that quality varied from park to park. Further, park superintendents sometimes expressed the wish that volunteers were more "controllable" (i.e., more predictable and dependable), but when the director and employees appreciate volunteer help, "success snowballs."

The parks service plans to expand its use of volunteers. An official noted that through the media and word of mouth, news of volunteer achievements can stimulate positive public perception of the parks. According to one official, successful volunteers are those who are treated the most like regular employees. Often more staff time and materials are invested in them than in other volunteers, and they are supervised more carefully, he says.

### Summary of Findings and Recommendations on Volunteer Programs in State Parks

Of the 30 delegates to a parks programs conference sponsored by the National Recreation and Park Association in January 1983:

□ only 18 percent thought enough time was being spent *planning* volunteer programs for national, state, and city parks;
□ only 33 percent said they used *job descriptions* for volunteers;
□ only 18 percent provided training for volunteers on a regular basis;
□ only 24 percent had procedure manuals for volunteers;
□ only 24 percent kept records of volunteer hours.[39]

None of the participants thought that enough time was devoted to evaluating volunteer work.

The state parks officials interviewed felt that volunteers needed more training, and several states were planning to ask for more money for this activity. Some officials also noted the need for training supervisors; not all supervisors worked well with volunteers. One official noted that the park supervisors who were most successful in using volunteers treated them like regular employees, expecting a lot from them and instructing them in their duties.

Volunteers are generally welcome in the parks system. They are used for a much larger percentage of the work in some parks than in others. It appears that the use of volunteers is on the increase.

The suggestions for selection of nonprofit volunteer agencies in Massachusetts, listed earlier in the discussion of volunteers, appear worthwhile for other states as well.

## PUBLIC-PRIVATE PARTNERSHIPS AND PRIVATE DONATIONS

Public-private partnerships take many forms. The main ones are reviewed briefly in turn.

### Leasing Facilities and their Operation

Another way in which the private sector helps share the responsibility of state parks is in leasing and donating land and facilities. Eleven directors of state parks report that their states lease historic structures to individuals and nonprofit groups. These arrangements have many advantages. Lessees, who usually provide routine care and maintenance, may contribute time, energy, and money for more authentic restoration than a state can afford. (Lessees may benefit from generous federal tax credits for privately financed landmark preservation.) Vandalism and arson, common problems in empty buildings, are reduced, thus saving administrative funds. And more people can enjoy park resources.[40]

### Land Trusts

Private land trusts often help states acquire land for parks. Thirty-two directors of state parks (64 percent) report working with trusts.[41] Land trust activity involving state parks is more prevalent in the Southeast. (The sluggish land market may have generated increased interest in donations with tax benefits.) The Cleveland office of the Trust for Public Land played a seminal role in creating Cleveland Lakefront State Park along the shores of Lake Erie. It identified opportunities to match private land donations and corporate contributions with limited state money. Local groups can make a special contribution because of their familiarity with personalities and politics.

### Sharing Resources

States, and state park systems, are creating new kinds of parks that weave together land and resources owned by several governmental land agencies and private landowners. A number of these parks are near urban areas where citizen pressure for preservation of green space is high but land is typically in mixed ownership and high in price.[42]

Partnerships between states and private entrepreneurs are providing new services in parks. In New Hampshire, where skiing revenues pay for a major part of the state parks' operating costs, a private business will build and operate a new base lodge at the foot of the skiing area in Mount Sunapee State Park, turning over a portion of its profits to the state. The director of the Massachusetts Division of Forests and Parks predicts an increasing public-private mix in the upkeep of state parks.[43]

Five parks in Dallas are protected by Turtle Creek PARKnership, Inc. The Dallas Park and Recreation Department recently created an endowment for the care of this belt of parks. Community organizations and citizens, including former First Lady, Lady Bird Johnson, joined to raise $3.5 million for the endowment. Earnings will go toward improved park maintenance, new sculptures and fountains, horticultural displays, and free concerts.[44]

### Land Conservancies and Contributions

Additional state land that can be used for recreation is acquired by purchase, donation by a private party or organization, or the state's acquiring the right for citizens to use it.

New York, New Jersey, and Connecticut, which plan for additional open space as a tri-state region, all have legislation in place and executive policies that promote temporary and permanent preservation of privately owned open space using regulation, tax policy, cooperative arrangements, and other-than-fee acquisition.[45] Sometimes land, such as a golf course, is preserved for the use of only certain fee-paying citizens; at other times, the land is open to the public. Landowners sometimes trade rights for dollars or tax abatements, or special districts are created. In the case of the 1 million-acre New Jersey Pinlands National Reserve, one-third of the total acreage is in public ownership and two-thirds is private.[46]

Many private foundations and other private contributors add

land to state parks and recreation areas. Nonprofit land conservancies and land trusts lead private sector involvement in open space preservation. In the tri-state region alone, more than 70 land trusts and small conservancies own or protect more than 32 square miles of land, sometimes for a fraction of fair market value. Preserves of larger nonprofit organizations such as The Nature Conservancy and national and state Audubon Societies add 37 square miles of protected open space, and private nature centers add another 24 square miles. Most of these areas, however, are not attached to state parks.[47]

Foundations and contributors helped create and develop the 700-acre Olompali State Park in Marin County, California. The California State Park Foundation helped raise acquisition funds. Because the state park system lacked funds to develop a management plan, the San Francisco Foundation matched citizen-raised dollars to pay for one by a private consultant.[48]

**Summary of Findings and Recommendations on Private Sector Involvement in State Parks**

In addition to the traditional use of concessions, the most successful and rapidly expanding ways to deliver services in state parks appear to be through volunteers and an important recent development, the organization of special, often incorporated, groups to receive and funnel donations of land to the parks.

CONTRACTING AND CONCESSIONS

Contracting for maintenance activities such as garbage collection in state parks appears to be more efficient than using state employees, especially as park use increases. Contracting for linen service and leasing concessions for specialized services such as food, boating, horseback riding, and fishing also seem to be cost competitive, though few detailed cost comparisons have been done.

Generally, state parks should contract or franchise concessions when they cannot find trained employees to provide a service or when needed services cannot be delivered because of a job freeze. The seasonal nature of park services indicates that contracting is often appropriate, but with a core of dedicated state employees supervising all contracting. All contracts should contain performance standards, and they need to be monitored carefully, with periodic formal performance evaluations.

An apparent trend in the use of contracting and concessions in state parks is the increased number of contracts or concessions held by nonprofit groups. Groups concerned with the special care of certain park resources, such as historic sites and buildings, may initiate these agreements.

### VOLUNTEERS AND NONPROFIT GROUP HELP

The use of state park volunteers adapts well to many services. Volunteer service in a park probably has more glamour and adventure than service in other settings. The Boy Scouts, Girl Scouts, senior citizen clubs, and other groups can enjoy their "work" in the company of friends.

Using volunteers can create problems for public employees, especially when volunteers replace public employees. For example, it has been reported that replacement of some seasonal government employees with volunteer workers lowered U.S. Forest Service staff morale.[49]

The states are not yet providing a consistent, appropriate amount of training and monitoring of volunteers, but they are working toward this goal. They are beginning to hire statewide recruiters and coordinators for park volunteers. Most park directors seem to think that volunteers are worth the trouble it takes to use them. However, volunteer training and responsibility vary markedly from park to park, more so than from state to state. This situation indicates the importance of the attitude of the park director.

Voluntarism in state parks may increase substantially if the work remains attractive. Volunteers appear to be plentiful. Although the states have turned to volunteers because of cuts in government funds coupled with increased park use, they have been happily surprised with the success of most volunteer programs.

A special problem caused by the use of volunteers came about because members of a group had especially strong biases about park uses. Members of a nonprofit group brought in by a Massachusetts park director to operate an environmental education program criticized state land management practices to visitors, surely inappropriate behavior when they were acting as surrogates for the state.[50]

Based on interviews and the literature on volunteering in parks, states that are not using volunteers or that have small volunteer programs should:

□ increase their use of volunteers,
□ budget for and set up more formal training programs for volunteers so that they can be more useful,
□ hire a statewide volunteer recruitment coordinator,
□ consider writing "contracts" with volunteers to indicate their level of responsibility, and
□ ensure that park volunteers are duly and publicly recognized for their contributions to society.

Agreements with nonprofit environmental groups, such as the Massachusetts Audubon Society, to provide services may improve quality as well as save money because of the groups' incentives. Some caution should be exercised when using these groups: the interests of *all* park clients should be preserved; in addition, volunteers must be reminded that they represent a state government when working with park customers.

## PRIVATE DONATIONS OF LAND

Another trend in the use of the private sector in parks is increased dependence on private donations, including sharing of land.

Donations of land to parks by private parties have a long history, but recently friends (citizen) groups have formed to receive the donations and expedite channeling the funds directly to the parks rather than to a state general fund. Other successful developments include several levels of government and citizens co-managing parcels of land that are made parts of state parks.

Private groups may have a distinct advantage over government agencies in arranging for land donations from private parties:

Proponents [of involving nonprofit groups in land acquisition] also claim that nongovernmental parties operating as public sector surrogates can establish better working relationships with landowners whose cooperation is often needed for effective management. Rather than reaching for the shotgun when the feds or the state shows up, landowners are more likely to work with individuals who are perceived as their neighbors.[51]

Involving the private sector increasingly in park land acquisition and park services seems to be beneficial to the parks and their users.

---

## Notes

1. The Conservation Foundation, "Paying for Parks: State Innovations in Dedicated Accounts and Trust Funds," briefing papers, 23 June 1986.

2. U.S. Department of the Interior, Heritage Conservation and Recreation Service, *Contract Services Handbook* (Washington, D.C., 1979), p. 8.

3. Ibid.

4. Ibid.

5. This section is based on telephone interviews with William Hopkins, Director, Delaware Division of Parks and Recreation, August 1987, and Charles Salkin, Manager of Technical Services, Division of Parks and Recreation, October 1987, and from documents received from them.

6. This section is based on a telephone interview with Mrs. Patricia Harrell, Administrative Assistant, Financial Management, Florida Park Service, Department of Natural Resources, October 1987, and from documents received from her.

7. Florida Division of Recreation and Parks, "Contractual Services Quarterly Report for Contracts Exceeding $3,000" [1987].

8. Ibid.

9. This section is based on a telephone interview with Mike Farmer, Business Manager, Parks Division, Florida Department of Natural Resources, 7 October 1987, and from documents received from him.

10. Information on contracting in South Carolina parks was obtained from a telephone interview with Leonard Jones, Director of Procurement, State Parks Division, South Carolina Department of Parks, Recreation and Tourism, October 1987, and from documents received from him. Information on South Carolina concessions is from a telephone interview with Jim King, Chief of the merchandising section of the South Carolina Department of Parks, Recreation and Tourism, October 1987.

11. This section is based on a telephone interview with Chuck Wyatt, Regional Park Superintendent, Division of Parks and Recreation, Virginia Department of Conservation and Historic Resources, October 1987, and from documents received from him.

12. Virginia Department of Conservation and Historic Resources, Division of Parks and Recreation, "Concession Study Results," 1987.

13. Ibid.

14. Ibid.

15. This section is based on a telephone interview with Dennis Konkol, Chief of Administrative Services, Bureau of Parks and Recreation, Wisconsin Department of Natural Resources, November 1987, and from materials received from him.

16. Wisconsin Department of Natural Resources, "Operation and Maintenance Agreement, Lucius Woods State Park," 12 June 1981.

17. Ibid.

18. Ibid.

19. Phyllis Myers and Ann Christine Reid, "State Parks in a New Era: A Survey of Issues and Innovations," The Conservation Foundation, 1986, p. 51.

20. Ibid.

21. Sute Mote, "Volunteers Carve New Trail Around Rim of Lake Tahoe," *The Sacramento Union*, 18 June 1987, pp. D14 to D-16; and *Fiscal Watchdog*, November 1986, p. 5.

22. "State Parks in a New Era."

23. "Volunteers Carve New Trail."

24. Ibid.

25. Karen Brown, "Adopt-a-Trail: A Progressive Partnership," in *Outdoors, Case Studies*, supplement to The President's Commission on Americans (Washington, D.C., 1986), p. 131.

26. Ibid, p. 55.

27. Ted Tedrick, William W. Davis, and Gerald J. Coutant, "Effective Management of a Volunteer Corps," *Parks and Recreation* (February 1984), p. 54.

28. Ibid., p. 57.

29. Steven L. Yaffee, "Evaluating the Role of Nonprofit Organizations in Providing Public Recreation Services: The Massachusetts Pilot Program. Summary Report" (Harvard University, June 1982) John F. Kennedy School of Government.

30. Ibid., pp. 81–84.

31. This section is based on telephone interviews with William Hopkins, Director, Delaware Division of Parks and Recreation, August 1987, Charles Salkin, Manager of Technical Services, Division of Parks and Recreation, and Bonnie Carmine, Administrative Officer, Division of Parks and Recreation, October 1987, and from documents received from them.

32. Volunteer reports supplied by Delaware.

33. This section is based on a telephone interview with Don Page, Administrator, Operational Resources, of the Florida Park Service, 2 October 1987, and from documents received from him.

34. Florida Division of Recreation and Parks, "Manpower Augmentation Report," 1 January–30 June 1986 and 1 July–31 December 1986.

35. Florida Division of Recreation and Parks, Volunteer Services Section, Florida Operations Policy Manual, rev. 1986.

36. This section is based on a telephone interview with Michael N. Hunt, Administrative Assistant, Division of State Parks South Carolina Department of Parks, Recreation and Tourism, October 1987, and from documents received from him.

37. Phyllis Myers, The Conservation Foundation, interview October 1987.

38. This section is based on telephone interviews with Chuck Wyatt, Virginia Department of Conservation and Historic Resources, October 1987, and with Mark Batista, Chief Interpreter and Program Coordinator, November 1987, and documents received from Mr. Wyatt.

39. "Effective Management of a Volunteer Corps," p. 58.

40. "State Parks in a New Era," p. 55.

41. Ibid., p. 56.

42. Ibid.

43. Philip Shabecoff, "Keeping State Parks Green as Federal Funds Dwindle," *New York Times*, 8 February 1987.

44. Sandra Matney, Acting Director, Dallas Park and Recreation Department.

45. *Case Studies*, pp. 12–13.

46. Ibid.

47. Ibid., p. 13.

48. Ibid.

49. Ibid., p. 20.

50. Steven L. Yaffee, "Public Sector Surrogates: Using Nonprofit Organizations to Provide Public Services," Paper presented to the Association for Public Policy Analysis and Management, 30 October 1987, p. 10.

51. "Evaluating the Role of Nonprofit Organizations," p. 16.

# Chapter Four

# USE OF THE PRIVATE SECTOR IN DELIVERY OF HUMAN SERVICES

*Keon S. Chi, Kevin M. Devlin, and Wayne Masterman*

Various forms of alternative service delivery are used for social services, but the majority are in the form of *contracts*. The entities with which state governments contract vary widely—private companies, nonprofit organizations, and educational institutions. Less frequently used are *grants and subsidies*, and *vouchers*. Occasionally states use *voluntarism* and *self-help* approaches as well.

This chapter discusses alternative service delivery methods in selected human services programs and assesses their success. Human services in state government are diverse in terms of programs available and client groups served. Here the focus is on the delivery methods most commonly used. Programs highlighted include day care for children, adoption, school dropout prevention, weatherization assistance, Medicaid, and mental retardation and mental health programs.

## *DAY CARE FOR CHILDREN*

In the last two decades, the demand for day care has risen along with the number of women entering the work force. The increasing need for day care to allow women in poor families to work led state government to enter the fray. Because day care is not a traditional service of state government and because there was no precedent on how states should handle it, the states met with little employee resistance as they began contracting with private providers for this service.

Contracting and voucher systems are the two most widely used service delivery methods. The following sections examine private sector involvement in Massachusetts, New Jersey, Pennsylvania, and California day care programs.

**Massachusetts' Day Care Partnership Initiative:**
**Use of Contracts and Vouchers**

*DESCRIPTION*

By 1980, 52 percent of all Massachusetts women were in the work force, so the need for increased and improved day care was becoming apparent.[1] The Governor's Day Care Partnership Initiative was launched in January 1985 to expand available day care. The program called for contracts and vouchers to create partnerships with the private sector to harness available resources to improve the state's approach to subsidizing care for low-income families. State spending for the initiative increased nearly 50 percent from fiscal year 1985 to fiscal year 1987, rising from $67.1 million to $101.1 million. Over 90 percent of the increase was allocated to day care services for low-income families or families in crisis.[2]

The Department of Public Welfare funds a *voucher* day care program operated by the Department of Social Services through an interagency agreement. It provides services to children of former welfare recipients who are either receiving job training in the Employment and Training Choices Program or are working in jobs found through that program. The program refers participants needing day care services for their children to private voucher management agencies that help them locate a day care center that provides the services that they desire. Parents pay the day care providers monthly with the vouchers plus a fee based on family income.[3]

Massachusetts also subsidizes day care through *contracts* with day care centers for low-income individuals who are working or seeking employment but are not participating in the voucher program. The Department of Social Services operates a contract day care program using a network of 12 child care resource and referral agencies. These agencies established 20 centers to provide information to parents wishing to participate in the contracted segment of the day care program. Some agencies operate more than one center. The role of resource and referral agencies is to provide information for parents to select the day care facility that best suits their needs. Families can also gain information through lists provided by the Office of Children and directly from day care providers.[4]

As of November 1987, the state contracted with more than 600 day care providers. Day care providers respond to requests for proposal (RFPs), and they must meet a set of predetermined standards. Each contract provides for a given number of slots reserved for children for a given number of days per year at a rate of compensation negotiated by Department of Social Services regional offices. Day care providers bill the state monthly for each child according to the number of days he or she attends.

Massachusetts subsidizes day care for more than 13,000 low-income children through contracts with day care centers and family day care systems. It also subsidizes day care for 4,000 children with protective, preventive, or other special needs under the Supportive Day Care Program.[5]

A family is eligible for basic day care if its gross family income is at or below 70 percent of the state median family income and the parents are either working or seeking work. Eligible families pay a fee based on their income for the first child and half that amount for a second child; care of a third child is free.

In addition to contracts and vouchers, Massachusetts uses *grants and loans*. New England Telephone allocated $750,000, for example, to provide capital improvement grants to private day care centers in Massachusetts. The state also created the nation's first and largest loan fund to stimulate employer investment in day care centers for employees. The Massachusetts Industrial Finance Agency (MIFA) established the Child Care Facilities Loan Fund in 1986 to make loans to employers interested in setting up or improving day care facilities for their employees.[6] The agency that implements the program is a quasi-public firm established by the state to foster economic development measures. It allocates funds using revenues from the sale of industrial development bonds for loans, but MIFA also recruits corporate sponsors to help fund day care projects.

*ASSESSMENT*

The state officials interviewed were satisfied with their several systems. From 1984 to December 1986, the number of licensed day care places for children grew by 15,058 places, or 15 percent, for a total of 112,971. As of October 1987, Massachusetts was subsidizing day care vouchers for 9,500 children of former or current Aid to Families with Dependent Children (AFDC) recipients participating in the Employment and Training Choices Program, a major increase over the 2,900 children subsidized in June 1985. The state subsidizes day care for an additional 13,524 low-income children through contracts with day care centers and family day care systems. Ninety-five percent of these children's families earned less than $10,000 a year in 1985.[7]

### New Jersey's Voucher Program for Day Care

*DESCRIPTION*

In 1982, the New Jersey Department of Human Services initiated a day care voucher program in Hudson County. Although under 1 percent of the entire budget for day care services is delivered through vouchers, the program is growing and the department is planning to use more vouchers in the future. Licensed day care centers and family day care homes participate.

Hudson County is an urbanized section of New Jersey adjacent to New York City. Among the reasons for implementing a voucher program here are a new emphasis upon parent choice, long waiting lists for day care, increased numbers of eligible children, and the goal of encouraging families to become more self-sufficient. The program is located in Hudson County because of the dearth of subsidized day care services in many parts of the county.

Parents must work or go to school to be eligible for the voucher program; they must also meet income criteria based on family size—$19,800 for a family of two, for example. The program is restricted to preschool children. Provider charges are negotiated with the state, and parents must pay any costs above those that the state pays. The state pays $25 a week for family day care in private homes, $37.50 a week at preschools, and $52.50 for infant center care.

The Department of Human Services office in Jersey City provides resource and referral services to parents. Parents may select any agency that they wish in Hudson County. Services outside the county are available for Hudson County parents who commute to other counties to work, but these parents are restricted to licensed day care centers outside Hudson County. Parents give vouchers to day care providers who present them to the Department of Human Resources offices in Trenton for payment. Parents and providers complete attendance sheets that are used to verify use of the services.

*ASSESSMENT*

The use of vouchers has increased accessibility of day care services, county officials believe. In Hudson County, children from 9 of 12 communities have received subsidized care for the first time because of the program. Parental involvement has increased, with parents selecting 59 percent of the centers and all the day care homes. The voucher system costs 25 percent less than the state's contracted day care system, and it is less expensive than state-operated centers, partly because of the absence of cost-of-living adjustments. Further, there are no start-up costs. The primary advantage of the voucher system, however, is that it provides immediate accessibility to services. Surveys of both providers and parents reflected broad satisfaction with the quality of services. All day care providers surveyed in 1987 said they would continue to participate. Of those parents surveyed, 93 percent liked the program.[8]

Yet the voucher program remains small. As of November 1987, only 112 children were participating in a program whose capacity is 180. The program had a six-month waiting period because of the many families in need of subsidized day care. Moreover, there were no plans to expand the program beyond Hudson County, partly because of the objections of contracted centers in the state, which opposed the competition for subsidized day care that broad implementation of a voucher system would bring.[9]

### Pennsylvania's Contracts and Vouchers for Day Care

*DESCRIPTION*

Pennsylvania provides day care services to families who need subsidies for such services. The state relies on a contract-slot system whereby the Department of Public Welfare allocates subsidized day care "slots" through contracts with providers. Allocation of funds is based on services delivered the previous year. The number of slots authorized in each contract is based on the likelihood that families in need of subsidized care will seek care from that provider. The state has only 123 contracts out of a total of 6,000 providers. Some are multisite contracts, so that more than 400 day care sites are covered. Providers serve the number of clients authorized in their contracts, and they bill the state monthly. State payments to providers are based on the units of service provided (i.e., the number of children served per day) and come from both state and federal funds. Parents' fees are based on income. The state frequently uses private agencies to deal directly with day care providers.[10]

Pennsylvania is considering a change to a service authorization system in which families who qualify for subsidies may select any day care provider that meets their needs. This change would move the state away from a contract system to a voucher-like system. This new approach has been tried in Lehigh County.

The features of the voucher-like program implemented in Lehigh County include:

- □ a neutral, private information and referral agency to serve all parents,
- □ the opportunity for all parents to select a licensed day care provider,
- □ a mechanism to verify attendance, and
- □ parental fee payments based on income.

The state selects private referral agencies on a noncompetitive basis and contracts with for-profit as well as nonprofit firms. The private local referral agency recruits providers and negotiates fees. Providers bill the agency for services, and the state, in turn, reimburses the agency for all costs incurred.

In 1984 and 1985, the Lehigh County program used a voucher system but abandoned it in 1986 because of the cumbersome paperwork involved.[11]

A feasibility study conducted in Allegheny County and information gained from programs in other jurisdictions indicate that alternatives to the contract system would open up the market and contain day care costs by enhancing competition. Clients no longer restricted to contracted facilities for services would be free to select facilities that meet their needs, thus motivating providers to compete for consumers by lowering prices. An alternative arrangement would also promote the state's goal of full use of all regulated facilities. Past studies also cite the advantages of a system that would combine the strengths of the contract and voucher systems.[12]

### ASSESSMENT

A study of the Lehigh pilot voucher program drew several conclusions. The voucher system, with a central information and referral agency to determine eligibility, reduced the average price per unit of service and consequently increased the number of slots available by 20 percent. Using a voucher book was unwieldy and inefficient; an authorization card and simplified methods of recording attendance and fee payments were preferable. The use of a resource and referral agency to determine eligibility for benefits was successful in expanding parental choice. Administrative fees amounted to approximately 7 percent of the total program costs. No impact on quality of service was detected.[13]

A 1986 consumer survey indicated that parents were acquiring new information about their options for day care services.[14] A second study reported that private day care facilities in urbanized Allegheny County, which includes Pittsburgh, were underused but that contracted facilities were fully used. The report concluded that a voucher program would be feasible in Allegheny County.[15]

As is common with subsidized day care, as of November 1987 Lehigh County had a waiting list of 120 children. A statewide voucher-like service authorization program could increase services 20 percent and significantly reduce the number of families waiting for service.[16]

### California's Alternative Payment Program

*DESCRIPTION*

California's Child Development Division of the Department of Education has developed an Alternative Payment (AP) Program whereby the state contracts with agencies that subcontract with county child care programs. A few of these AP agencies are public entities (e.g., school districts), but 52 of the 69 contractors are private nonprofit child care agencies. Both nonprofit and for-profit contractors are eligible to bid on contracts, which are awarded on a competitive basis. Eligible low-income families select a state-licensed child care provider; providers bill the AP program in the counties where they do business. The goal of the program is for parents to select day care arrangements that are best for them.

The AP contractor receives applications for assistance from parents and verifies their eligibility to receive assistance. Parents must demonstrate financial eligibility and testify that they are employed, in search of a job, enrolled in school, or physically or emotionally disabled.

The program ensures that day care providers are licensed by the state and that they retain copies of applications. Many AP agencies also provide resource and referral services to parents under separate contracts with the state. Parents can use these programs to obtain information at the beginning of their day care search and then return to the Alternative Payment Program to secure assistance.[17]

ASSESSMENT

With a budget of $25.7 million, about 8 percent of the California day care budget, the Alternative Payment Program provides for approximately 6,600 children. The program is less expensive than other state-funded day care programs, costing an average of only $15.87 per full-service unit per day, as opposed to $18.85 for other subsidized day care programs. Despite California's efforts in day care, the demand far exceeds the number of places available in state-subsidized centers. These efforts have been less expensive to the state than similar programs, but the waiting list has grown to several thousand.[18]

**Use of the Private Sector in Day Care Programs: Discussion**

Both contract and voucher systems allow state governments considerable flexibility in availing themselves of private sector ability to provide the service while conserving state resources. At the same time, and possibly even more important, alternative service approaches, especially voucher-like systems, allow clients to choose locations most convenient and satisfactory for them.

Much of the debate in this area in the coming years will concern the advantages and disadvantages of using vouchers rather than contracts—the strength of the former is client freedom of choice, with quality control the strength of the latter.[19] Massachusetts, New York, California, Illinois, and New Jersey are among the states that have instituted both systems—a route that may ultimately be the best one for other states.

---

## ADOPTION

Many children are not difficult to place, but some are, particularly minority and handicapped children and those older than 10. In some states, the number of minority and handicapped children in the care of the state is large, and these states have turned to private resources. This section describes experiments in Illinois and Kentucky.

**The Illinois One Church, One Child Program**

*DESCRIPTION*

In the area of special needs adoption, the Illinois One Church, One Child program is a most impressive state effort. It exemplifies an effective volunteer, self-help program combined with state deregulatory activities. George Clements, a black Roman Catholic priest, initiated the program.

In 1980, Father Clements became disturbed at the number of black children in foster care in Cook County. After urging his parishioners at Holy Angels Church to adopt black children, he set an example by adopting a child. Soon he gathered with other black clergymen to organize an effort whereby they would encourage their congregations to consider adoption. The goal was a simple one: at least one black family in each black church in Chicago would adopt one black child.[20] A Board of Ministers would coordinate a formal program among the churches. By using the black church to place black children, these clergymen were harnessing one of the most powerful resources in the black community, their care for each other.

The Illinois Department of Children and Family Services decided to help the One Church, One Child effort. The state secured a federal grant to fund the program and assisted the Board of Ministers by publicizing the effort and identifying children to be adopted. The board helped recruit adoptive parents for children who were particularly hard to place. When federal funding expired, the state funded the program; in fiscal year 1986, the budget included $84,000.[21] Planning and implementation are primarily the responsibility of the Board of Ministers and the pastors.

*ASSESSMENT*

Impacts of the One Church, One Child program are significant. In Cook County alone, the number of children awaiting adoption dropped from 702 in 1981 to 70 in 1986. The program saved the state more than $14 million in child care aid. However, how many of these adoptions are attributable solely to the program is an unknown.[22]

According to the Illinois program administrator, the Board of Ministers assists the state by gauging public opinion on state adoption policy. The state relaxed some requirements for adoptive parents, such as homeownership, partly because of feedback received from the board. Further, the state responds more quickly to inquiries. When it was discovered that many black families attempting to adopt were disillusioned at the slow response they received, the state accelerated the process, contacting every family recruited within 48 hours, meeting with them within two weeks of recruitment, and completing preparation services within three months.[23]

The state provides training to other states considering One Church, One Child programs.

### Kentucky's Special Needs Adoption Program

*DESCRIPTION*

Special needs children are particularly hard to place. The Kentucky Department of Social Services established its Special Needs Adoption Program (SNAP) in 1978 to recruit adoptive parents in anticipation of the requirements of the federal Adoption Assistance and Child Welfare Act of 1980. SNAP became a statewide program in July 1980.

SNAP contracts with local private nonprofit agencies to increase the number of adoptions. For example, the Louisville Urban League recruits black families to adopt black children, provides placement services, and helps train and provide postadoption services to families. In Hopkinsville, a private nonprofit community action agency, Pennyrile Allied Community Services, provides similar services.

The state releases competitive RFPs for these contracts. The commissioner of the Department of Social Services must give final approval of all contracts before they are authorized. Contractors bill the state monthly for costs incurred in providing services up to the maximum amount specified by the state agency.

SNAP and the local media cooperate in publicity (marketing) efforts. Profiles of adoptable children are shown on local television newscasts in Louisville and Lexington, and a column entitled "Kentucky's Waiting Children" is printed in more than 30 local newspapers as part of the media's voluntary effort to help recruit parents for hard-to-place children. Kentucky recently established a One Church, One Child program as part of its adoption effort.[24] The staffs of each program are small, only two people per office.

SNAP had placed 667 special needs children as of July 1986. Moreover, its minority recruitment efforts resulted in placing 60 percent of the black children referred to the program. However, a growing proportion of SNAP referrals are blacks—the percentage awaiting referral rose to 38 percent in late 1986 in a state whose black population is only 12 percent.[25] Clearly, more extensive efforts to place these children are needed.

### ASSESSMENT

Relatively small numbers of children have been placed by the Louisville and Hopkinsville programs. But the director of contracting for social services is pleased with the services provided to adoptive families in addition to recruitment and placement—for example, helping parents in adjusting to their role as adoptive parents.

The state received few bids on the Louisville contract, resulting in a less competitive contracting process than the state would like. A contract with the Lexington Urban League was not renegotiated because of its poor placement record; once again, the state is the sole provider of minority recruitment services in the Lexington area.[26]

---

## DROPOUT PREVENTION

Increasing numbers of students across the country drop out of school. In Oregon, one out of every four high school students drops out.[27] These youth lack many of the skills that employers require; the result is that taxpayers may well have to support them through welfare and other services. A new activity that illustrates potential opportunities in this emerging area of state concern is described below.

### Oregon's Grant and Public-Private Partnership Program for Student Retention

### DESCRIPTION

The National Governors' Association estimates that for every dollar spent on dropout prevention, the taxpayer saves $9. Mindful of this figure, Oregon's governor pledged during his election campaign in 1986 that he would attack the school dropout problem. Two days after he began his term in 1987, the governor launched Oregon's Student Retention Initiative with help from the private sector. The initiative is designed to identify at an early age those students who are in danger of becoming dropouts and to help them before they leave school.[28]

The initiative provides grants to private agencies and school districts to initiate programs in partnership with the state for at-risk youth. Some of the programs focus on education, but many are for teenage parents and for counseling on drug and alcohol abuse and other problems. Private organizations are particularly involved in drug and alcohol programs.

The Youth Coordinating Council, an agency that funds local youth initiatives in education and job training, makes recommendations for Student Retention Initiative policy and grants awards. Local planning groups comprised of teachers, youth counselors, representatives from business firms, and community leaders review and discuss youth needs in their communities. The program emphasizes public-private partnerships in decision making in each community.[29]

The Oregon Legislature allocated more than $8 million for the initiative for fiscal years 1987–89. Approximately $4.6 million is used for competitive grants awarded to community agencies that develop program proposals to keep young people in school. Individual awards are $30,000–60,000. The $4.6 million consists of $2.3 million in federal Alcohol and Drug Funds, $865,000 in federal Employment Training Funds, and $1.5 million in state general revenue funds.[30]

In July 1987, the first grant awards were made to 34 school districts and other organizations in 21 counties. Local efforts include drug and alcohol counseling, training in social and academic skills, tutoring, parenting skills classes, and vocational training.[31]

Private agencies being funded include the Phoenix School of Roseburg, which provides remedial education services using federal Job Training Partnership Act funds. The Jefferson Council of Alcoholism, Inc. provides counseling for teenage alcoholics. In-Between, Inc. works with youth who have a high risk of becoming dropouts and provides remedial education services and counseling as well as clothing and medical care as needed.

### ASSESSMENT

According to one member of the Youth Coordinating Council, the strength of this effort is that the many actors in the process—state agencies and local private and public agencies—cooperate to make the process a successful one. The private sector, recognizing that the school dropout is a community problem, has contributed time, facilities, and high-tech equipment. An effort is being made to develop an evaluation system.[32]

---

## WEATHERIZATION ASSISTANCE:
## KANSAS'S WEATHERIZATION GRANT PROGRAM

State governments commonly use federal funds to help the poor weatherize their homes. In 1977, the U.S. Department of Energy (DOE) began a program of weatherization assistance to low-income families. In 1982, additional funding was made available through Low Income Energy Assistance Program (LIEAP) block grants. Kansas's Weatherization Grant Program is an example of the private sector's helping provide weatherization assistance.

### DESCRIPTION

Since 1982, the Kansas weatherization program has received all its funding through the DOE and LIEAP programs.[33] The Kansas Department of Social and Rehabilitative Services allocates grants to private agencies (and some local governments). They, in turn, use these funds to process client applications, authorize work on homes of eligible recipients, and ensure that the homes receive all the materials they need. Clients are served in all 105 Kansas counties.

Of the 12 agencies receiving grants from the state, 8 are private, nonprofit agencies, including several community action agencies. The other 4 are city or county government agencies and similar public entities. Subgrantee agencies may not be for-profit. The state no longer uses a competitive RFP process because it generally awards funds to the same agencies each year. Some serve several counties, covering large regions of the state.[34]

Allocation of funds to private agencies is based on the percentage of eligible persons in the area of jurisdiction. Agencies are required to make periodic financial reports to the state, including the number of homes weatherized. Weatherization services include caulking, weatherstripping, replacing windows and doors, and minor repairs to roofs, walls, and furnaces. State officials inspect homes prior to allocation of funds and after the work is performed to verify that funded services are completed satisfactorily.[35]

### ASSESSMENT

DOE recognized Kansas's weatherization program as one of the nation's best in 1981, when the state received the ninth largest supplemental award among the states based on the number of homes weatherized in 1980–81. Residents of more than 40,000 low-income homes received assistance between 1977 and 1985, including more than 15,000 elderly persons. The average spent on each house is approximately $1,500. DOE estimated that weatherization has reduced fuel consumption 14 percent. Kansas estimated that, as of 1985, only one out of every six eligible households had received assistance through the program.[36]

## MEDICAID: KENTUCKY'S CONTRACT WITH ELECTRONIC DATA SYSTEMS

Several states use private contractors as fiscal agents to process or pay vendor claims on behalf of agencies delivering Medicaid services. These firms include such different types of organizations as Blue Cross and Electronic Data Systems (EDS).[37] Kentucky's contract with EDS provides a good example.

### DESCRIPTION

In 1983, officials in Kentucky's Cabinet for Human Resources concluded that a fiscal agent's processing Medicaid forms would be more efficient than continuing with state personnel. Lower salaries were one of the ways in which cost savings could be realized, for example. In July 1983, Kentucky contracted with EDS after issuing an RFP and using competitive bidding. Kentucky recently signed a new contract with Electronic Data Systems Corporation. Scheduled to begin in July 1988, it was signed on the condition that EDS meet certain performance standards. For example, the company's investigation of fraud will be assessed by the use of indicators of individuals' excessive use of Medicaid services.

EDS retains staff in Frankfort to process Medicaid claims. Doctors and other providers of Medicaid services send claim forms directly to the EDS offices in the capital. The EDS staff processes the claims, basing payments on state policies. (The state sets compensation for each type of medical or dental procedure.) EDS supplies data through its main computer in Dallas, which is connected with its Frankfort office. Transactions are put on computer tape, which is sent to the state Treasurer's office, which processes and distributes checks. EDS receives 50.75 cents per claim.

### ASSESSMENT

EDS has dramatically improved the delivery of Medicaid services in Kentucky, according to the Department of Medicaid Services. The company has a 99 percent claims accuracy rate. Further, claims are settled in an average 3–4 days, compared to 15 days prior to EDS involvement.

In 1983, the state estimated cost savings of $1–1.2 million per year. Cost savings were not considered in negotiating the new contract because of the great expense that the state would incur if it were using its own staff and computer equipment. That the state needed to contract for Medicaid payment processing was a foregone conclusion.[38]

---

## MENTAL RETARDATION AND MENTAL HEALTH FACILITIES

Greater use of the private sector in providing mental health and mental retardation services holds great potential. Contracting with private providers is increasing as more private for-profit and non-profit organizations become involved in working with state governments to provide services that were traditionally the exclusive responsibility of the public sector.

There are almost no examples of contracting for the total management and operation of a facility, but there are many examples of specific services being delivered by private providers.

Services being contracted for, or for which contracting is being considered by state mental health service officials, include: facility management, new construction, medical services (i.e., physicians, nurses, occupational therapists, physical therapists, dentists), vocational training, vocational rehabilitation, counseling, maintenance, data processing, in-house training, pharmacy, security, transportation, food service, laundry, and cultural and religious programs. The services most often contracted for are medical and dental care, pharmacy, food and laundry services, maintenance, construction, and transportation. Community treatment operations are also frequently contracted for. The deinstitutionalization of the past two decades has significantly increased the demand for community-based services, and the private sector often fills the need.

A 1986 inventory of facilities for the mentally retarded conducted by the U.S. Department of Health and Human Services reported that of the approximate 4,200 intermediate care facilities in the United States, only 21 percent were owned and operated by the public sector. The remainder were owned and operated by the private sector, 31 percent by for-profit organizations and 48 percent by nonprofit firms.[39]

One factor important to note regarding the above statistics is the size of the facilities. Approximately 320 of them have a 100-plus bed capacity. Of that number, the public sector was responsible for 70 percent. The remaining 30 percent was divided equally between the for-profit and nonprofit organizations.[40]

These statistics do not take into account the management or operation of public facilities by the private sector, which would add to the proportion of facilities being operated by private firms.

Discussed below are two major types of contracting: the management and operation of mental retardation and mental health facilities, and the management but not the operation of these facilities.

### Contracting for Management and Operation

Although most states rely on contracting to purchase clinical and support services, few contract for both management and operation of either a state mental health or mental retardation institution. We reviewed the efforts of six states in their attempts to contract for these operations. Thus far, only three are considered successful.

The desire to reduce costs is a principal but not the only reason that states consider this approach. Physical plant replacement or rehabilitation, pressure from patient advocacy groups for improved conditions and treatment, staff recruitment needs, reduction of the state government labor force, and legislative and political reasons are among the many rationales for this step.

Kentucky, Florida, and South Carolina have contracts with the private sector to operate and manage a state facility. The state objectives in contracting differ considerably.

## KENTUCKY DESCRIPTION

Since 1975, the Commonwealth of Kentucky has contracted for management and operation of the Outwood Mental Retardation Facility in Dawson Springs. Its purposes were to reduce costs, alleviate a professional staff recruitment problem in rural southwestern Kentucky, and achieve accreditation. Res-Care, Inc. is the current, but not the original, contractor for this 80-bed facility. The state constructed a new facility adjacent to an outmoded complex that previously served as a Veterans Administration Hospital. The Res-Care contract is for one year, with two one-year renewal options.

The original contracts contained cost-saving incentive clauses in which the contractor could gain additional fees (or have its fees reduced) if the costs for the year were less than (or greater than) the contract target cost. Each contract for 1975 through 1981 contained a cost-savings sharing arrangement in which a target price was specified and the for-profit contractor received a percentage of the savings below that price. The contractor received all cost savings from 1 percent to 10 percent of the contract's target cost, one-half of all savings from 10 percent to 13 percent, 25 percent of savings from 13 percent to 15 percent, and none beyond 15 percent of the target cost. Limiting the incentive to the first 15 percent of savings, the state felt, would discourage cost-cutting efforts that could adversely affect service levels.[41]

## KENTUCKY ASSESSMENT

Under the contract, the Outwood Mental Retardation Facility was accredited by the Accreditation Council for Services to Mentally Retarded (ACMRDD) and certified for Medicaid reimbursement. The state finds service quality quite satisfactory. Per diem costs have been reduced since contracting commenced, and Outwood consistently reports lower costs than the three state-run intermediate care facilities for the mentally retarded (ICF/MR) in Kentucky. State records indicate 1983 per diem costs at Outwood of $85 and 1986 costs at $86. These cost savings were achieved despite the fact that since 1984, the contractor has not had the incentive option. Kentucky dropped the option because of possible effects on quality of service.[42]

*FLORIDA DESCRIPTION*

In Florida, the need for physical plant replacement and pressure from patient advocacy groups were among the stimuli that prompted state officials to contract for the management and operation of a cluster of facilities for the mentally retarded. The legislature had passed a law mandating the state purchase of health and rehabilitation services whenever possible. This requirement provided the opportunity for the replacement of two large ICF/MRs with 26 cluster facilities, most of them under contract to private operators.

Florida contracted with eight private providers to deliver services to the mentally retarded in the cluster facilities, each with a cluster cottage patient capacity of 24 persons. All but four were managed and operated by the private sector. Regardless of whether services were contracted for, this clustering proved more costly: economies of scale were lost because of both capacity and siting. Costs increased from $96 per day per patient (approximately $35,000 per year) to $120–132 per day per patient (approximately $44,000–48,000 per year). After operating the four noncontracted cluster facilities for one year, the state determined that it was less expensive to contract for them. Among the private sector organizations delivering cluster facility management and operations are Res-Care Inc., Life Concepts Inc., Sunrise Inc., ARA Services Inc., and the Anne Stork Center.

These contracts typically run one year, with options for renewal for another two years. The rationale for this short time is that many state statutes prohibit the expenditure of funds not yet appropriated. Although the requests-for-proposals or requests-for-bids may be issued only once every three years, the state can bind itself for only one budgetary period.

*FLORIDA ASSESSMENT*

Florida officials are satisfied with the quality of care provided. The contractors provided better trained staff, better equipment, and more new technology than did the public sector. In addition, the downsized institutions facilitated the provision of higher quality care and the monitoring process.[43] It is easier now to get state funds.

## SOUTH CAROLINA DESCRIPTION

In South Carolina, a private firm, P.H.P., Inc., operates a 200-plus-bed multiuse facility. It includes geriatric care skilled nursing services. South Carolina contracted with P.H.P. for one year, with an option for renewals of up to an additional four years. The state retains the quality assurance and security functions and funds the renovation and leasing costs for the physical plant.

## SOUTH CAROLINA ASSESSMENT

Reduction of the state work force was a primary motivator for contracting. As a result, the state reduced its payroll by $2.4 million. Additionally, it avoided replacing more than $1 million in needed equipment and supplies.[44] The contractor improved use of Medicaid-certified beds, resulting in securing larger Medicaid reimbursements.

### Unsuccessful Attempts to Contract

Tennessee, Idaho, and New Hampshire had unsuccessful experiences in implementing contractors for operation of mental health or mental retardation facilities.

In 1982, Tennessee issued an RFP to contract for the Lakeshore Mental Health Institute, a 570-bed hospital, hoping to improve service and reduce costs. Tennessee laws require three responsible bidders to award a contract, but only two companies submitted proposals. Officials cited two possible explanations for the low level of response. One was that the supply of providers was not large enough. The second was that the rigid conditions set forth in the RFP and in the enabling legislation discouraged potential bidders. The conditions required that all state employees be retained by the contractor at their present compensation levels for nine months and that the contract be limited to one year, after which it would be rebid with no possibility for an automatic renewal.

New Hampshire was thwarted in 1983 in its negotiations with potential providers to contract for building and operating a 150-bed mental health complex. The state demanded that the director of the facility be a state employee and that all contractor personnel report to that person. The bidders would not agree to that stipulation.

In Idaho, a commission was established in 1981 to study the feasibility of contracting for operation of a state mental retardation facility. The Idaho State School and Hospital for the Developmentally Disabled was identified as the facility to be contracted. The private providers who investigated the proposal determined that the facility could not be operated efficiently because of the condition and design of the physical plant.[45]

### Contracting for Facility Management but Not Operation

States might opt to contract for the management but not the operation of a state mental health facility—that is, replace the state employee management team with private sector managers while retaining the state employees to operate the facility. Typical endeavors use 4–15 individuals as the management staff. These persons may be or may not be on-site. The contract often divides the compensation to the contractor between salaries and fees. Fees may be tied to performance.

*FLORIDA DESCRIPTION*

In 1981, a private firm, Amerimanage, Inc., contracted to supply the management teams for Northeast Florida State Hospital near Jacksonville and South Florida State Hospital near Fort Lauderdale. South Florida State Hospital had more than 1,300 patients with a wide variety of needs. The facility had not been certified by Medicaid/Medicare or by the state health department. Eleven hospital directors had been appointed and removed in as many years, and forensic clients had escaped. There had been grand jury investigations of these matters as well as others, including patient abuse.

Amerimanage provided an 11-person management team. It included the chief administrator, a director of financial services, a director of quality assurance, a community relations and patient advocacy director, a forensic unit director, and a clinical director. The plan was to phase out gradually the private on-site managers and replace them with state employees. In 1987 the phaseout was completed.

In 1984 Amerimanage was given a contract for the management of Northeast Florida State Hospital. The problems here were not as extensive as in the previous case, but they included charges of patient abuse and neglect. This management team consisted of an administrator, deputy administrator, and training director. The cost for this one-year contract with one one-year renewal was $350,000, including both salaries and management fees.

## FLORIDA ASSESSMENT

The Amerimanage team was judged successful in accomplishing tasks that had previously eluded state employees. South Florida State Hospital was successfully certified by both Medicare/Medicaid and the state health department. The staff-to-patient ratio was increased from 0.8:1 to 1.6:1, and new facilities were approved. To accomplish this improvement, however, the cost per patient per day almost doubled, from $65 to almost $120. The budget remained constant over two two-year periods. The contractor made physical plant improvements, improved the staffing ratio, and expanded services.

### Opportunities in Mental Health Programs

Contracting is the most common option for making greater use of the private sector in the mental retardation and mental health fields. The costs to the state for mental retardation and mental health programs are significant, and the expertise outside the public sector is credible.

Although the operation and management of state hospitals for the mentally ill is a high-cost and high-priority issue, not much contracting is done. More experiments and careful monitoring and evaluation of contracts is needed to determine the feasibility of using the private sector more for mental illness facilities. In regard to care of the mentally retarded, some experimentation suggests that contracts can be productive.

---

## SUMMARY FINDINGS AND RECOMMENDATIONS FOR HUMAN SERVICES

The authors preface this section by noting that in many states, many human services are delivered by local governments, with state agencies acting primarily as over policymakers. The recommendations below apply primarily to state agencies that have delivery responsibility.

### Contracts

Contracting in human services has become a well-established practice over the years. A national survey conducted in 1971 revealed that 25 percent of social services were purchased. By 1979, the figure was 55 percent.[46] Contracting will likely continue to be widely used in the delivery of social services. Four specific recommendations are in order:

1. Obstacles to contracting, such as the opposition of public employee unions and the stress of making the transition from one kind of service delivery to another, are fewer in this area than in some other areas because the provision of many social services is relatively new. For example, states have only grappled with delivery of Medicaid services since 1965. Provision of day care services, as highlighted in this chapter, is also relatively new. If states do not have a long history of providing services to people and are adding or expanding a service, it is easier to make the transition from state-provided services to private provision of services. In most states, both nonprofit and for-profit private organizations are eligible, though use of nonprofit firms is more common in human services.

2. Two principal advantages of contracting with private organizations are an avoidance of the bureaucratic complications commonly found in public organizations (e.g., rules, regulations, public employees unions) and the opportunity to introduce competition as a way of reducing costs. But only through competitive bidding can both advantages be realized.[47] Competition motivates contractors to offer lower bids, thus lowering government costs. Competitive bidding is relatively new—and uncommon—in many human services contracting efforts.

3. Requirements should be laid out clearly for contractors in the state RFPs, including required services, any necessary timetables, and bid evaluation procedures. The emphasis of any statement of work should be oriented toward results and not merely the process by which they should be achieved. An impartial committee should be formed to evaluate the proposals and select the one that would best fill the state's needs.[48] Costs should not be the sole consideration in selecting a contractor; the likely quality of service, as indicated by such elements as each bidder's plan of action, should be carefully scrutinized. Renewal of contracts should be based, at least in part, on past performance.

4. Contracting is not restricted to private agencies or companies. Services may also be provided by local governments. They, in turn, may subcontract with service providers.[49]

## Grants and Subsidies

Grants to many nonprofit human service agencies do not require an extensive bureaucratic apparatus, and they are a relatively simple form of alternative service delivery. They are generally politically feasible as long as measures are taken that prevent funds from being squandered by their recipients. Grants can be used as seed funding to help establish programs. After a program's first year, it can rely on its own funding.

Grants to private organizations may be awarded on a competitive basis. These competitions, as distinct from competition for contracts, are usually among proposals that offer somewhat different services to somewhat different groups of clients. Grant competitions seldom focus on cost as a major criterion. We suggest that grant applications be subject to careful examination of both costs and likely service quality, especially when grant renewals are possible.

If a grant program provides one-time funding only, the need for extensive monitoring is reduced because the recipients are not eligible for additional funding. But some measures of individual program effectiveness should be established to ensure that the funds are used effectively.

Careful monitoring of program effectiveness is always important, especially when grantees are eligible for renewals, to ensure that the public is adequately served.

## Vouchers

The states have been increasing their use of vouchers in human services delivery. The chief advantage of a voucher system is that an individual client can choose the individual vendor that provides the kind of service and location that best meet his or her needs. Voucher systems are not inherently cost savers, but they can reduce costs to the government when the government sets the prices for different levels of service and the clients select vendors whose level of service is lower than that which the government had previously provided them. This situation is common with day care vouchers, for example. On the other hand, cost savings can be offset by more clients' applying for the vouchers because of their accessibility to services. A disadvantage of vouchers compared to contracts is that contracting permits greater opportunity for quality control.[50] The voucher system is common in the provision of day care.

Four specific observations about the voucher system follow:

1. The voucher system works best under certain conditions:[51]
   - □ People's preferences for a service differ significantly, and the differences are legitimate.
   - □ Individuals are motivated to shop aggressively for the service.
   - □ Individuals are well-informed about market conditions, including the cost and quantity of the service and where it can be obtained.
   - □ Many suppliers of the service are already in competition, or is it a relatively easy field to enter.
   - □ The quality of the service is easily determined by the user.
   - □ The service is relatively inexpensive and is purchased frequently, so the user learns by experience.
2. Voucher systems can take several different forms. In a true voucher system, the client receives a voucher from the state or its management agency that he or she uses to pay the provider. The service provider in turn redeems the voucher from the state. In many voucher systems, clients sign up with providers and providers then bill the state or the management agency that has contracted with the state. In yet another type of voucher system, the state pays the clients directly and the clients then pay the providers.[52] Further, clients may use identification cards to acquire a service from providers, whereupon the latter are reimbursed by the state. Medicaid commonly uses this form of the voucher system.
3. Service quality concerns are alleviated when clients are restricted to state-licensed facilities for acquisition of a service (common for day care). Periodic surveys of client satisfaction should be conducted to ensure that service is adequate. The voucher system is being used experimentally for delivering selected human services in several states, especially day care. The effectiveness of each voucher program is determined by the form of voucher selected for each program and the degree to which basic economic prerequisites are met. Voucher systems using direct payment to clients or service providers are apparently less cumbersome than using a payment book.
4. Day care and some other services are more feasibly carried out through the voucher system than others. Other potential opportunities for the use of vouchers are for various mental health and

other counseling services (perhaps alcohol and drug abuse counseling) and even residential care facilities for income-eligible clients. There is little experience with these services, so efforts should be considered experimental.

**Volunteer and Self-Help Approaches**

The volunteer and self-help approaches are not widely used in state human services programs though they are at the local level. Following are our summary findings and recommendations:

1. Volunteer efforts seem to work best when they originate with private initiatives and the state joins an effort that has been launched. An example is Illinois's One Church, One Child program. Nevertheless, there is no fundamental reason why state agency officials cannot take the initiative to encourage the private sector to help.
2. The most feasible volunteer programs are those begun by churches, community groups, and other private organizations. Again an example is the One Church, One Child program.
3. Volunteer systems are potentially useful in the human services area, but skilled volunteers to fill needs are difficult to find. Volunteer programs are potentially popular with public officials.
4. The recommendations on the use of volunteers in chapter 3, on parks and recreation, apply to human services:
   □ provide adequate training to both the volunteers and the supervisors who use volunteers.
   □ keep track of the performance of volunteers to ensure that they appear when scheduled and perform well.
   □ treat the volunteers as if they were employees, with expectations that they will perform well;
   □ provide for recognition of individual volunteers; and
   □ use some form of central volunteer office that can help recruit volunteers, match volunteers to job descriptions, help train supervisors, and help provide recognition.

---

## *CONCLUSION*

State experiences indicate that contracting and vouchers are often effectively used in the delivery of human services. State government can tap resources beyond its own. Moreover, alternative service delivery sometimes saves a good deal of money. State governments use contracting and other forms of alternative service delivery to launch programs quickly and contain the growth of bureaucracy. Over the past two decades, human service agencies at all government levels have routinely contracted with nonprofit organizations and made contracting part of the political landscape.[53]

Yet state policymakers and administrators in human services should give careful consideration to cost savings and quality of service. Whether private agencies can meet equity standards as would a welfare agency is especially pertinent. Use of private, for-profit firms may tempt these firms to cut service for expensive, hard-to-help clients if contracting and monitoring procedures are inadequate. Use of private, nonprofit public welfare organizations can create an equity concern if they are unevenly distributed throughout the state; individuals similarly situated in all respects except their residential location could have different access to public benefits. Equity needs to be a specific factor when states consider using the private sector for alternative service delivery.

---

## Notes

1. Massachusetts Office of Human Resources, "Final Report of the Governor's Day Care Partnership Initiative," June 1987, p. ix.

2. Ibid.

3. Ibid., pp. x–xiv.

4. Tracey Abrams, Voucher Program, Massachusetts Department of Social Services, telephone interview, December 1987.

5. Joyce Sebian, Deputy Director, Day Care Policy Unit, Massachusetts Department of Social Services, telephone interview, November 1987.

6. "Final Report of the Day Care Partnership," p. xiii.

7. Ibid.

8. Barbara Catterall, Director of the Hudson County Day Care Voucher Program, New Jersey Department of Human Services, telephone interview, November 1987.

9. Ibid.

10. Pamela Brewitt and Patricia C. Broderick, "Subsidized Day Care: Advantages and Disadvantages of Alternative Delivery Systems" (Villanova University, 1987), pp. 12–13.

11. Irene Molzan, Pennsylvania Department of Public Welfare, November 1987.

12. Pennsylvania Legislative Budget and Finance Committee, "Report on a Performance Audit of the Administration of Pennsylvania's Subsidized Child Day Care System," September 1987, pp. 32–36

13. "Subsidized Day Care," p. 7.

14. Irene Molzan, telephone interview.

15. The Conservation Company (Philadelphia), "Evaluation of Lehigh County Voucher Subsidized Day Care Program," Pittsburgh, 1986, p. 1.

16. Irene Molzan, telephone interview.

17. California Department of Education, Child Development Division, "Program Facts for 1986–87," 1987, p. 11.

18. Patricia Gardner and Richard Wheeler, California Department of Education, Child Development Division, telephone interviews, October and November 1987.

19. "Subsidized Day Care," p. 20.

20. Illinois Department of Children and Family Services, "One Church, One Child: Implementing a Minority Recruitment Program," March 1987, p. 4.

21. Larry Weintraub, "Adopt-Child Plan to be Expanded," *Chicago Sun-Times,* 27 February 1986, p. 14.

22. Ibid.

23. Gary Morgan, Associate Deputy Director, Program Operations, Adoptions, Chicago Office, Illinois Department of Children and Family Services, telephone interview, November 1987.

24. Kevin M. Devlin, "State Adoption Programs for Children with Special Needs," *CSG Backgrounder,* The Council of State Governments, November 1986.

25. Kentucky Department of Social Services, "Summary Project Description, Kentucky One Church, One Child Black Adoption Program," 1986, p. 10.

26. Nancy Bruner-Wilson, Department of Social Services, Kentucky Cabinet for Human Resources, telephone interview, November 1987.

27. Oregon Department of Human Resources, "Reducing the Dropout Rate: Oregon's Student Retention Initiative," August 1987, p. 1.

28. Ibid.

29. Ibid., p. 2.

30. Ibid.

31. Oregon Youth Coordinating Council, "Oregon Model Youth Programs," May 1987, pp. 1–25.

32. Nita Crimmins, Oregon Youth Coordinating Council, telephone interview, November 1987.

33. Kansas Department of Social and Rehabilitative Services, "Overview of the Low Income Energy Assistance Program and the Weatherization Program," December 1985, pp. 21–22.

34. Ibid.

35. Ibid., p. 25.

36. Ibid., pp. 25–27.

37. Keon S. Chi, "Medicaid Cost Containment through Third-Party Liability Programs," *Innovations*, The Council of State Governments, August 1984, p. 5.

38. Mark Birdwhistle, Assistant Director, Department of Medicaid Services, Kentucky Cabinet for Human Resources, telephone interview, November 1987.

39. A. Sirrocco, National Center for Health Statistics, "The 1986 Inventory of Long-Term Care Places: An Overview of Facilities for the Mentally Retarded," Advance Data From "Vital and Health Statistics, No. 143," DHHS Pub. No. (PHS) 87–1250, Public Health Service, 1987, Hyattsville, Md., p. 5.

40. Ibid.

41. Harry P. Hatry and Eugene Durman, *Issues in Competitive Contracting for Social Services* (Falls Church, Virginia: National Institute of Governmental Purchasing, 1985), pp. 18–19.

42. Ibid., p. 20.

43. Virginia Department of Planning and Budget, "The Feasibility of Contracting in Virginia's Mental Health and Mental Retardation Facilities," 1987, pp. ii and 1–5.

44. Ibid.

45. Ibid.

46. Ibid.

47. "*Issues in Competitive Contracting*," p. 19.

48. Ibid., p. 24.

49. "Subsidized Day Care," p. 4.

50. Ibid., p. 20.

51. E. S. Savas, *Privatization: The Key to Better Government* (New York: Chatham House, 1987), p. 113.

52. "Subsidized Day Care," p. 2.

53. Michael Lipsky and Steven Rathgeb Smith, "Providing Social Services Through Nonprofit Organizations" (Paper presented at the 83rd Meeting of the American Political Science Association, September 1987, Chicago), p. 34.

# Chapter Five

# USE OF THE PRIVATE SECTOR IN EMPLOYMENT AND JOB TRAINING

*Keon S. Chi and Kevin M. Devlin*

State employment and training programs frequently target groups that have a high risk of unemployment and that need assistance in the form of welfare or unemployment insurance benefits. Much employment training focuses on retraining workers who risk displacement because of outmoded skills. Retraining is one element of an extensive effort to retool U.S. industries and keep them competitive in the world market. Some training programs are designed to serve the growing population of at-risk youths—teens who drop out of school and enter the job market without skills, thus risking chronic unemployment.

State agencies use several alternative methods to provide employment and job training services. The most common form is *contracting*. State governments contract with both for-profit firms and nonprofit organizations for employment and training services. Sometimes *vouchers* are provided to allow individuals to select the training programs that they need. *Grants* and *subsidies* to providers of services are also used. Other approaches, such as *voluntarism*, are not common.

This chapter highlights examples of the private sector's providing employment and training programs for state governments. Clients are of three types: displaced workers from traditional industries, individuals dependent on welfare, and high-school dropouts. The states attack the problems of severe unemployment and mismatched skills and jobs in a variety of ways.

## TRAINING FOR DISPLACED WORKERS

Several states have developed programs that focus on retraining workers who need to develop new skills so that they are employable. Such programs may serve workers who are in danger of losing their jobs, but they emphasize helping the unemployed. This section briefly describes the use of grants and vouchers in Illinois and performance contracts in California.

### Illinois's Grant and Voucher System Used by the Prairie State 2000 Authority

*DESCRIPTION*

Since January 1986, Prairie State 2000 Authority has been the cornerstone of Illinois's effort to retrain displaced workers. This agency is charged with development of innovative job retraining programs as part of the state's economic development plan.[1] The legislature established the agency in 1983 in response to unemployment resulting from the recession of 1981–83. Prairie State 2000 is especially concerned with upgrading the skills of workers to help them adapt to advances in technology and other changes in the work place. A small staff (four individuals) administers a streamlined application process that is said to make the assistance it provides relatively accessible to employers.[2]

Prairie State 2000 consists of two programs: the Employer Training Assistance Program (ETAP) and the Individual Employment and Assistance Program (IEAP). Of the 10,000 who have received retraining since 1983, nearly 75 percent were trained through ETAP.

ETAP provides financial assistance to Illinois companies through *grants* and *loans* that help cover training costs for employees who need technical retraining. Companies must show a financial need to be eligible for assistance. Applications are approved by the agency's seven-member board, which includes the state Treasurer, the directors of the Department of Commerce and Community Affairs and the Department of Employment Security, and four gubernatorial appointees who are subject to approval by the Senate. ETAP provides grants covering up to 50 percent of the cost of an approved training program and loans covering all those costs.

ETAP grantee companies are paid half the amount of their grants at the beginning of their programs. Companies receive the other half when they have a pool of trainees who have been retained for at least 90 days in work for which they are retrained.

IEAP provides job training *vouchers* to individuals who need to improve their skills or develop new ones. These people apply for assistance through Prairie State 2000's Chicago office, the companies or schools from which they would like to receive training, or their unions' headquarters. Unemployed workers may receive vouchers for up to $2,000 to cover the full costs of training, and employed workers are eligible for vouchers for up to $1,000 to cover half the training costs. There are no restrictions on where a client is retrained. Many grant recipients select their current work places or local community colleges as training sites.[3]

Grants and voucher funding are available for training for any type of job. For example, training is provided in such diversified tasks as making compact disks, removing asbestos from older buildings, and using computers. One of the largest IEAP grants was made to Caterpillar, Inc., which received nearly $400,000 to help train 13,000 workers at various Illinois plants. Excluding this project, the average grant is about $17,000, and the median number of employees trained at each site is 80.[4]

### ASSESSMENT

Employers retained ETAP trainees for at least 90 days at a rate of 96 percent of 1986; IEAP's placement rate was 65 percent. No systematic evaluation was conducted, however, to assess what would have happened without the program. Training costs averaged $140 per individual for ETAP and $650 for IEAP. For each dollar spent by the state in ETAP, private companies spent $7.75.[5]

According to the head of the Prairie State 2000 Authority, program success is encouraged by the requirement that providers' proposals specify the types of training to be implemented and by use of site visits to verify compliance with their plans. The state believes that limited resources are producing good results for workers and employers.[6]

### California's Performance Contract for Employment and Training

### DESCRIPTION

The California legislature established an Employment Training Panel (ETP) in 1982 to initiate an employment and training program. The objectives are to encourage job creation, reduce employer unemployment insurance costs, and satisfy employers' needs for skilled labor. The program provides skills training to unemployment insurance claimants, particularly recent recipients of unemployment insurance benefits who have exhausted their benefits, and workers who are likely to be displaced if they are not retrained.[7] The state uses a portion of its unemployment insurance funds to support this effort.

Funds are allocated to private sector employees who argue to the state's satisfaction that they cannot afford to assume the full cost burden of a training program. As in Illinois's grants program, full reimbursement for training expenses is permitted only after an employee has been hired and retained for 90 days and at a wage approved by ETP. The performance contract approach in California, however, is an "all or nothing" program. Advances for program grantees may be arranged, but funds must be returned to ETP for any trainees who are not permanently placed.

The panel, which is comprised of gubernatorial appointees, considers training plans and proposed budgets presented by applicants in determining how much aid should be allocated to each of them. The amount of assistance varies, but the average amount allocated per recipient employer was $500,000 during fiscal year 1986–87, when more than $51 million in aid was distributed to companies.[8] A wide variety of agencies and firms have applied for and received assistance, including banks, manufacturers of high-tech goods (e.g., computers), colleges and universities, labor unions, and private businesses.[9]

California does not use competitive bidding for these grants. According to program officials, the primary reason is the fear that competitive bidding would discourage potential participants. The state has not considered using *vouchers* for employment and training programs. Individuals, according to the executive director, are poorly equipped to find appropriate jobs because of "poor information."

ASSESSMENT

The California contract program has enjoyed some success. A total of 600 contractors have participated. As of July 1987, 60,000 individuals had enrolled, 11,000 had not completed training, and 23,500 were placed in jobs within 90 days—about 48 percent of the persons who completed training. ETP's 1986 analysis showed that employees' earnings increased an average of 55 percent after training, from nearly $14,000 a year to more than $21,000. Moreover, the average number of weeks of unemployment per year decreased from 5.6 to 2.1 for participants.[10] The extent to which improved economic conditions, as distinct from the training program, may have been responsible for these improvements, is not known.

In the past, allocation of training and employment programs involving private funds was based on the number of enrollees for training, not the number subsequently hired for paid jobs. In addition, employment and training were based at local schools, and the programs were not flexible enough to adjust quickly to changes in the job market.

The executive director of the Employment Training Panel believes that ETP has been successful mainly because of the performance contract approach. Companies are motivated to provide training only when it prepares participants for available jobs in the companies. Compensating training providers only for successful job placements is crucial in ensuring program success.[11]

### Summary Assessment of the Illinois and California Programs

Both programs link the amount of assistance to subsequent performance. Efforts like these motivate employers to provide effective training, and they discourage signing up large numbers of workers simply to acquire funds. These programs enable companies and sometimes employees to contract with training agencies of their choice, allowing recipients of funding flexibility.

---

## TRAINING FOR WELFARE RECIPIENTS

States often use employment training to help welfare recipients out of poverty. The programs attempt to break the cycle of dependency on welfare by giving workers marketable job skills. Such efforts can pay for themselves through savings to taxpayers. Together, state governments and the private sector are beginning to deliver the types of training that offer bona fide opportunities to clients.

### Massachusetts's Contracting for Employment and Training

*DESCRIPTION*

One of the nation's most well-publicized efforts to provide training opportunities is that in Massachusetts. The Employment and Training Choices Program (ET) has operated since 1983. It offers welfare recipients various choices as to the type of assistance they may receive, including career planning, adult literacy and education classes, college course work, direct assistance in job placement, supported work, and job skills training.[12]

Services are delivered through performance-based contracts with providers of training services. Employers are permitted to secure these services through subcontracts with training providers.

Contractors are reimbursed only for those trainees who are hired full time, whose wages exceed the wage floor of $5 an hour, and who are on the job for a minimum of 30 days. Moreover, several performance-based contracts provide incentives for contractors to hire ET participants in jobs that pay considerably more than the wage floor.[13]

As of November 1987, about 200 contractors and subcontractors were participating in the program. Most are nonprofit organizations, including the State Employment Service, Job Training Partnership Act (JTPA) agencies, Bay State Skills Corporation, community action agencies, and neighborhood associations.[14] Competitive bidding is not used. ET graduates work for American Telephone and Telegraph, Wang Laboratories, and United Parcel Service, for example. In a supported work program, participants with little recent work experience are placed at private sector work sites where they learn work skills and gradually move into full-time employment. The program stresses graduated responsibilities, peer support, and close supervision to ensure a smooth transition to self-sufficiency.[15]

For the most part, Massachusetts does not use vouchers or any other alternative methods to provide training programs.[16] A small voucher program is used in the General Education Development Program.[17]

### ASSESSMENT

The ET program has enjoyed some measurable success since its inception in October 1983. More than 40,000 graduates of ET were employed by more than 8,000 employers by 1987. The average starting salary of full-time placements exceeded $13,000 during the first quarter of fiscal year 1987, a figure that is twice as high as the average family's Aid to Families with Dependent Children (AFDC) benefits.[18] Of those who went off welfare and through the program, 86 percent were still off welfare one year later. In early 1987, the Department of Public Welfare estimated that ET kept the AFDC caseload from growing; in December 1986, approximately 85,000 were on the AFDC rolls, compared to 88,000 in 1983. Without ET, as many as 100,000 would have been on AFDC.[19]

The state estimates that it saved more than $100 million in calendar year 1986.[20] A special study reported that the program saved far more than it cost.[21] As of mid-1988, about 200 state employees were working for ET.

This program does not use competitive bidding and does not emphasize the number of people participating. Instead, it focuses on the quality of services—providing clients with adequate wages and fringe benefits, including insurance benefits. Through performance-based contracting, the program focuses on results: jobs and wages.

Massachusetts has used competitive bidding in contracting for employment training in other programs. An official in charge of the program's contract management suggested that state officials consider competitive bidding as a better long-term approach than sole source contracting.

### Michigan's Opportunities and Skills Training Program

*DESCRIPTION*

The Michigan Opportunities and Skills Training Program (MOST), administered by the Department of Social Services, is based on a philosophy similar to that of the Massachusetts program. Upon receiving public assistance, individuals whom the state determines able to work are required to register for MOST. They can sign up at local welfare offices. More than 500,000 registered to take part in the program during fiscal year 1986.

MOST includes job search training as well as on-the-job training, and it uses private providers. In fiscal year 1987, about 44 percent of the $8 million spent on MOST was allocated to private sector programs.[22] MOST includes vocational education and training programs run by private nonprofit agencies as well as by public schools and colleges. They are contracted with to provide instruction in business, public services, and technology in a classroom setting.

For example, a Detroit area firm teaches skills to help participants qualify for jobs in the hotel and restaurant businesses, filling positions ranging from cooks to waiters and waitresses. Contractors are required to have placement services available to trainees.[23]

Another MOST program, the Community Work Experience Program (CWEP), targets those with little job experience. CWEP assignments to work sites of private and public employers are for six months and participants receive no wages, but they are given an opportunity to develop work habits and upgrade job skills while gradually adapting to work place conditions. The program provides community services, including day care services for clients' children, on a contractual basis. On-the-job training programs are occasionally used.[24] Contracts are performance-based in that contractor compensation is based on the units of service provided (e.g., the number of days of training per person). For job placement contracts, however, the contractor is compensated only for those individuals who are successfully placed.

*ASSESSMENT*

Since its inception in 1985, MOST has placed more than 100,000 welfare recipients in full-time jobs. The savings in welfare costs attributed to MOST are estimated at more than $570 million in the past three years. In fiscal year 1986, the average starting wage of individuals placed through contracts was $4.70, with about 17 percent earning more than $6 per hour. More than 4,500 persons were placed through contracts in fiscal year 1986. In fiscal year 1987, 24,601 public assistance cases were removed from Michigan's welfare rolls. By 1987, more than 20 states initiated similar employment training programs.[25]

**Connecticut's "Middleman" Contract Approach**

*DESCRIPTION*

In recent years, some states have contracted with firms to provide placement services to welfare recipients. In 1985, Connecticut's Department of Income Maintenance contracted with America Works, a for-profit firm, to carry out a three-year experimental project in the Hartford-New Britain area; the contract was extended through 1991. The objective is to help AFDC clients make the transition from public assistance to employment.

America Works recruits AFDC recipients through television and newspaper advertisements, mailings, and job fairs as well as through a Job Connection Program in the state Department of Income Maintenance. America Works maintains a booth in the state welfare office in Hartford, where individuals can request information and enter the program. Individuals can also sign up at the America Works office in Hartford.

Once clients enter the program, the firm matches their abilities with the needs of employers whom they have recruited. Employers interview potential trainees at least once before offering them a supported work position. When participants take such a position, America Works pays their salaries for up to four months of training.[26]

Under the supported work program, clients are closely supervised and their work responsibilities and pay gradually increase. The firm pays recruits $3.35 an hour to start, and after gradual wage increases over the training period, the recruits' welfare allowances are decreased to reflect their new income. America Works is required to work with employers who provide benefits.[27]

The goals for trainees are full-time jobs with their employers after the four months of training and complete separation from the welfare rolls.

America Works also provides preemployment preparation programs, including instruction on how to prepare for a job interview. Representatives regularly visit work sites to help trainees surmount any difficulties that might prevent them from completing training. America Works is compensated for its services by both fees from employers and state appropriations.[28]

ASSESSMENT

About 30 percent of participants have jobs in the clerical, maintenance, banking, health care, and restaurant fields.[29] Although America Works says that it maintains an active marketing program, the level of placement in the program has been low. During the first year of the program, 1985–86, America Works placed 122 participants, about 72 percent of its goal.

A state employee reported that America Works "could significantly increase its capacity to match the abilities of participants and the requirements of jobs."[30] From March 1986 to September 1987, 383 of 615 applicants (62 percent) were placed in supported work positions, but only 144 individuals (38 percent) were retained. In September 1987, 67 individuals were in supported work programs.

America Works had a similar contract with Ohio, but it was canceled. The state Controlling Board cited unacceptably high costs per trainee and America Works would not accept a two-month contract while the company's program was being examined. Local officials also opposed a private firm's profiting from helping welfare clients. Such objections also led to the demise of an America Works program in the Dayton area.[31]

---

## EMPLOYMENT AND TRAINING PROGRAMS FOR YOUTH

Some states target employment training efforts at individuals with a high risk of chronic unemployment or welfare dependency, particularly the young. Such youths are characterized by their lack of achievement in school and by a lack of knowledge on how to find a job. A high percentage of this group of youth is from low income or minority backgrounds, teenage parents, and high school dropouts.[32]

### Youth Employment Training Grant Program in Oregon

#### DESCRIPTION

In September 1983, Public/Private Ventures (PPV), a nonprofit organization in Philadelphia, helped implement a demonstration project in Oregon to develop a comprehensive strategy regarding the delivery of employment services for at-risk youth. The State Employment Initiatives for Youth (SEIY) program is based on two premises: that coordination of services for at-risk youths (e.g., education, employment training, social services) can lead to more effective service delivery and that states can play a vital role in delivering those services. PPV helped Oregon launch its program by providing an on-site coordinator to assist in administration.[33]

In the SEIY approach, state funds are allocated to the Youth Coordinating Council (YCC), which in turn gives grants to private and public agencies to support exemplary local programs. The membership of YCC consists of gubernatorial appointees representing state agencies that work with disadvantaged youth, key local leaders, and representatives of the private sector. YCC completes a needs assessment, develops a strategy for improving youth services, and selects local programs for funding.[34]

In Oregon, the YCC meets monthly. The Department of Education is its lead agency. Oregon has strong local government, and the chair of its YCC, a county commissioner, is said to be strongly committed to local control of services.[35]

The council uses a competitive request-for-proposal process that requires private and public sector applicants for grants to demonstrate that their programs serve specific target populations and participate in operations and financing by a variety of local agencies; further, there must be clear evidence of local ability to sustain council-financed projects. Grants serve as seed money to help private organizations and school districts launch their programs. They are not intended for long-term funding.[36]

The Oregon YCC supports a wide variety of local endeavors targeting the needs of at-risk youth, including remedial and alternative education programs as well as vocational education and training. Recipients of funding include community colleges, school districts, community organizations and agencies, and businesses participating in JTPA activities.

For example, the Vocational Options Project provides vocational training to disadvantaged youth through a multifaceted program whose alternatives to clients include job training combined with attendance at a local high school or an alternative education program. The program is a cooperative effort of several public and private entities, among them private employers and training agencies and local school districts.[37]

### ASSESSMENT

The YCC has exceeded its goals for job placement and number of youths served. With emphasis on decentralized planning, local officials can tailor programs to local needs.[38] Generally speaking, private contractors are doing a better job in teaching job skills and placement, and local schools are more successful in on-the-job training. Officials report that additional incentives may be needed for more active participation by private firms.[39]

---

### SUMMARY FINDINGS AND RECOMMENDATIONS ON EMPLOYMENT AND JOB TRAINING

#### Contracting, Grants, and Subsidies

States use grants, loans, and other kinds of subsidies to help companies implement job training assistance programs. Many state officials do not seem to distinguish between grants and contracts. Generally, the same types of recommendations apply to both.

Grants and contracting are the most common forms of alternative service delivery for employment and training programs. The state offers money to potential grantees or contractors to carry out its training objectives. The state then determines which applicants can best help achieve its objectives at a reasonable cost. We offer the following recommendations:

1. Because state governments have not been involved in extensive training using their own resources, the transition from state-provided to vendor-provided services presents a few problems. An important first consideration is establishing legal authority for grants or contracts by legislative action (as in Illinois and California). Doing so prevents any ambiguity about whether the state may establish a program. Additionally, states should decide whether both for-profit and nonprofit groups are eligible for grants and contracts, what to do when providers fail to perform, whether incentive contracting can be used, and who are the program targets—displaced workers, the unskilled poor, disadvantaged youth, or all three groups. Programs need to be tailored to the individual needs of each client group.
2. The grant or contracting process should be competitive. The states should set performance standards such as "desired" placement quotas to be achieved. The states should publicize grant and contract proposals through advertisements in business sections of newspapers. More active recruitment of possible providers is desirable. Both for-profit and nonprofit firms should be allowed to participate, but preference should be given to employers with job vacancies available for trainees.

   State governments should also evaluate each applicant's proposal on the basis of whether the type of training offered will help prepare participants for available jobs, whether the applicant can help participants secure jobs, whether the recipient's firm is financially sound, and what the costs are. Grants and contracts should specify the role of the provider in helping to secure jobs for participants as well as the amount of compensation that a provider will receive for each participant who completes training and is hired full-time.
3. The states should conduct on-site visits to training locations and check employment records of those who were trained. The states should verify the fact that those who were trained and hired were retained at their new places of employment; this verification procedure should be specified in the training agreement. Regular re-

ports by providers and evaluations by participants during training may be a good way to ensure the quality of training and to help motivate contractors.

4. A good measure of the effectiveness of many of these programs is the number of people who are permanently employed full time. This is the measure used by California, which contracts for training services to displaced workers, and other states. In predicting cost savings, states should consider the savings in welfare costs and unemployment benefits for trainees who receive permanent placements (defined by Illinois and California as retention of an employee for 90 days or more). Some states may feel that a minimum retention period longer than 90 days should be specified. For some programs (e.g., those for youth) the level of education completed, improvement in competency, and other measures of performance are needed.

5. The use of private resources to achieve public goals for employment training appears an effective alternative to states' providing these services on their own. If a company operates its own training program, it has considerable incentives to deliver high-quality training. Both employees and contractors are additionally motivated if they are fully compensated only for the expenses of trainees who are permanently employed. Emphasis on placement of participants encourages program quality. The use of incentive contracts whose final payments are contingent on placement of clients is relatively widespread in employment and training programs. They are effective.

### Vouchers

Vouchers are not common in the delivery of employment training services. Under a voucher system, a government sacrifices some of its discretion to the client. Voucher systems can be cumbersome and the state may lose some of its capacity to regulate training.

Individuals can use vouchers to purchase training services from vocational schools, community colleges, other educational institutions, or private companies. Vouchers allow more client choice, but the states may find it more effective to narrow client choices to training programs that are likely to lead to employment. Two specific recommendations are as follows:

1. Again, because state governments have not done a great deal of training in the past, displaced state workers are not expected to

object to a voucher program. Legislative authorization of such a plan, as stated in the first recommendation above, gives the program a sound legal base. The principal questions in setting up voucher programs are who is eligible to receive vouchers and what training programs clients may use. If a program targets welfare recipients, income levels can be used to determine eligibility. The state should authorize only qualified vendors to provide services to voucher recipients. This requirement sacrifices some of the individual's discretion, but could strengthen service quality.

2.  In the typical voucher system, the recipient pays the training provider with a voucher issued by the state. The provider, in turn, presents the voucher to the state for payment. Use of vouchers in this manner can be cumbersome, and it can cause the state problems in ensuring the right kind of training. It is probably better for the state to compensate providers directly for their services. Under this procedure, the client selects the vendor and the vendor requests payment from the state. In this way, the state can enforce performance standards through reimbursing trainers only for clients who complete training and/or achieve permanent (90-day minimum) placement. Voucher programs should be publicized through state welfare and unemployment offices so that both potential clients and vendors are aware of their availability. Participation should be encouraged, but probably should be made voluntary, for the recipients of public assistance or unemployment benefits. Clients who decide to participate will be more motivated than those who are forced to do so. The Massachusetts Employment and Training Choices Program is based on this philosophy.[40]

---

### Notes

1.  Illinois Prairie State 2000 Authority, "Background Paper," 1986, p. 1.

2.  Illinois Prairie State 2000 Authority, "Questions and Answers," 1986, pp. 1–4.

3.  Illinois Prairie State 2000 Authority, "Fact Sheet," 1986, pp. 1–2.

4.  "Questions and Answers," 1986, p. 3.

5.  Kristine Coryell, Chief Executive Officer, Prairie State 2000, telephone interview, October 1987.

6. Ibid.

7. State of California. SB 13, AB 828, 1982. Enabling legislation for the Employment Training Panel.

8. California Employment Training Panel, "Report to the Legislature," November 1986.

9. California Employment Training Panel, "Update on Panel Training Projects," July 1987, p. 72.

10. Ibid., pp. 29–30.

11. Steve Duscha, Executive Director, California Employee Training Panel, telephone interviews, October and November 1987.

12. Massachusetts Department of Public Welfare, "The Massachusetts Employment and Training Choices Program: Program Plan and Budget Request, FY 88," February 1987, pp. 12–13.

13. Ibid., pp. 13–14.

14. John Lanigan, Director of Research, Massachusetts Department of Welfare, telephone interviews, December 1987.

15. "Massachusetts Employment and Training," pp. 12–13.

16. Paul Beinheimer and Tim Reagan, Contract Management, Employment and Training Choices Program, Massachusetts Department of Public Welfare, telephone interviews, November 1987.

17. Tom Sellers, Assistant to Commissioner for Finance, Massachusetts Department of Public Welfare, telephone interviews, December 1987.

18. "Massachusetts Employment and Training," p. 1.

19. Ibid., p. 8.

20. Ibid., p. 1.

21. Massachusetts Taxpayers Foundation, "Training People to Live without Welfare," August 1987, p. 11.

22. Charles Valk, Michigan Department of Social Services, telephone interview, November 1987.

23. Ibid.

24. Michigan Department of Social Services, "Michigan Opportunity and Skills Training (MOST) Program," January 1987, p. 5.

25. John Herbers, "Job Training Efforts in Massachusetts and Michigan Move Poor off Welfare," *New York Times*, 30 March 1987.

26. Abt Associates, Inc., "Evaluation of the Supported Work Program: Interim Evaluation Report," 18 March 1987, pp. 71–73.

27. Ampero Garcia, Client Analyst, Job Connections Unit, Connecticut Department of Income Maintenance, telephone interview, November 1987.

28. Brenda Kaulback, Connecticut Department of Income Maintenance, telephone interview, November 1987.

29. Tom Condon, "State Finds Job Program That Works," *Hartford Courant*, 19 May 1987, p. B1.

30. Brenda Kaulback, telephone interview.

31. "Cleveland Works," *Cleveland Plain Dealer*, 10 August 1986, p. 4E.

32. David Gruber and Frazierita Davidson, "State Employment Initiatives for Youth: An Assessment of the Demonstration," Public/Private Initiatives, Philadelphia, November 1986, p. 1.

33. Ibid., p. 2.

34. Ibid., p. 3.

35. Ibid., p. 11.

36. Oregon Youth Coordinating Council, "Oregon Youth Today: 1986 Annual Report," pp. C-1 to C-5.

37. "State Employment Initiatives," pp. 32–33.

38. John Pendergrass, Oregon Youth Coordinating Council, telephone interview, October 1987.

39. Oregon Youth Coordinating Council, telephone interview, December 1987.

40. Robert D. Behn, "Managing Welfare, Training, and Work: Some Lessons From ET Choices in Massachusetts" (Paper presented at the annual meeting of the American Political Science Association, September 1987, Chicago), p. 3.

# Chapter Six

# USE OF THE PRIVATE SECTOR FOR STATE GOVERNMENT PASSENGER VEHICLE MAINTENANCE

*Mark Fall*

The management of state passenger vehicles is an often overlooked support service, but as costs for repair and replacement of passenger vehicles have risen, the use of the private sector has gained increased attention. For purposes of this discussion, passenger vehicles are those whose primary use is the transportation of state personnel on state business. They do not include heavy equipment, police vehicles, buses, and other types of vehicles whose primary use is not transportation of state personnel.

Fleet management is composed of two tasks:

☐ Maintenance of the vehicles—this task includes a) preventive maintenance, designed to prevent the need for repair (e.g., oil changes, balancing and rotating tires, tune-ups, checking brakes), b) routine repair of minor damage that can be completed expediently (e.g., replacing headlights, replacing tires, installing new belts), and c) major repairs, which require extensive time and effort to complete (e.g., body work, engine repairs, transmission repair). It also includes establishment of preventive maintenance cycles and oversight of repair warranties.
☐ Management of the passenger vehicle fleet—this task includes the deployment and assignment of vehicles and the analysis of information on the cost and quality of the fleet in the field. It often includes a computerized management information system (MIS) that provides the data needed.

This chapter focuses primarily on the first aspect of fleet management, maintenance of vehicles. It also discusses the importance of MIS in making determinations about the cost and quality of maintenance.

## SERVICE DELIVERY ALTERNATIVES

Traditionally, states have handled fleet maintenance in one of two ways. In the first, each government agency manages its own vehicles. The responsibility for maintenance of the fleet rests with each agency. In the second, a central agency purchases and maintains all vehicles, assigning them to other agencies. In either case, state-operated garages may be used for some or all repairs and services. States usually use private maintenance providers on an ad hoc basis for repairing vehicles without any contract arrangement, particularly for major repairs that cannot be made easily in-house.

Of the alternative service delivery approaches, only contracting has been used extensively. The scope of contracting varies dramatically across the country. Delaware, with the assistance of The Urban Institute and The Council of State Governments, in 1987 completed a national survey of contracting of fleet management services by state governments.[1] The results are shown in exhibit 6.1. Of the 49 states contacted, 11 contracted for at least some portion of their fleet maintenance. The number of vehicles covered by the contracts ranges from Hawaii's contract for maintenance on 200 vehicles to Illinois's for 11,000. The kind of maintenance contracted for, and the types of vehicles covered by the contracts, also varies. For example, Arizona contracted only for preventive maintenance on its passenger vehicles and heavy equipment, but Colorado contracted for all maintenance on its passenger and other vehicles.

The Urban Institute conducted in-depth interviews with representatives of four of the states contracting for fleet maintenance services (New York, Pennsylvania, Ohio, and Michigan) to examine their systems in detail and their use of MIS to track vehicle maintenance costs.[2] These states showed marked differences in the ways that they had arranged and used contracted services. (See exhibit 6.2)

A number of issues need to be considered in an analysis of the different forms of contracting and their effects. They are:

1. Type of contract
   □ length of the contract,
   □ whether it is bid competitively,
   □ how prices are determined, and
   □ use of performance or incentive contracts.

Exhibit 6.1 EXTENT OF STATE CONTRACTING FOR FLEET MAINTENANCE SERVICE

| State | Known extent of contracting[a] | Progress on developing management information system |
|---|---|---|
| Alabama | None[b] | Unknown |
| Alaska | Preventive maintenance, minor repairs on 300 passenger, heavy vehicles | Prototype mainframe |
| Arizona | Preventive maintenance on 1,500 vehicles, including 400 passenger cars | Prototype; PC |
| Arkansas | None | Wang VS system: mainframe, mini-computer |
| California | None | In-house, mainframe |
| Colorado | All maintenance for 1,000 passenger and other vehicles | Customized package, AT&T PC |
| Connecticut | None[b] | Unknown |
| Delaware | None | |
| Florida | None[b] | Unknown |
| Georgia | None[b] | Unknown |
| Hawaii | Maintenance of body, fender, glass and upholstery on central fleet of 200 cars | In-house program, IBM and Xerox, personal computers |
| Idaho | None | In-house, IBM hardware, mainframe |
| Illinois | All maintenance on 11,000 vehicles | Looking into it |
| Indiana | None | No system |
| Iowa | None | In-house, IBM hardware, mainframe |
| Kansas | None | In-house software, Univac hardware, mainframe |
| Kentucky | None[b] | Unknown |
| Louisiana | None[b] | Unknown |
| Maine | None[b] | Unknown |
| Maryland | None[b] | Unknown |
| Massachusetts | None[b] | Unknown |
| Michigan | Agreement with McCullagh Leasing to provide some preventive and routine maintenance on passenger vehicles; vehicle operators' choice to use authorized dealer, local repair facility, McCullagh, or state-operated garages | In-house, Burroughs mainframe |
| Minnesota | None | No system |
| Mississippi | None | No central system |
| Missouri | None | No system |
| Montana | None | Mainframe |
| Nebraska | Some contracting for certain vehicle parts | In-house, IBM hardware, mainframe |

Exhibit 6.1 *Continued*

| State | Known extent of contracting[a] | Progress on developing management information system |
|---|---|---|
| Nevada | None | Computerized fleet analysis; IBM PC, EP hardware |
| New Hampshire | None[b] | Unknown |
| New Jersey | None[b] | Unknown |
| New Mexico | None[b] | Trying to acquire system |
| New York | All maintenance on 6,000 passenger vehicles; agency choice to use in-house repair facilities | In-house, mainframe |
| North Carolina | None[b] | Unknown |
| Ohio | Preventive and routine maintenance only on passenger vehicles; major repairs done by specialized vendors; limited use of state garages | Implementing MIS |
| Oklahoma | None | In-house software, mainframe, IBM System 3G |
| Oregon | None | Implementing system |
| Pennsylvania | "Agreements" with 400 private vendors for performance. Also has one small state garage | In-house, IBM mainframe, personal computers |
| Rhode Island | None[b] | Unknown |
| South Carolina | None[b] | Unknown |
| South Dakota | None | Developing system |
| Tennessee | None[b] | Unknown |
| Texas | None | No central system |
| Utah | None | In-house software; WANG hardware; mainframe and PC |
| Vermont | None[b] | Unknown |
| Virginia | None[b] | Unknown |
| Washington | Preventive maintenance and minor repairs on 1,100 cars, vans and light trucks | Informational, mainframe |
| West Virginia | None[b] | Unknown |
| Wisconsin | None | In-house software, Microdata hardware |
| Wyoming | None | In-house, IBM hardware, AT&T terminals, mainframe |

Source: Telephone surveys conducted by The Council of State Governments and The Urban Institute during the spring of 1987.

[a]States that contract for maintenance also customarily have some state facility(ies) where repairs can be done in-house if an agency chooses.

[b]States not interviewed in sufficient depth to be sure they use no contracting for fleet maintenance. Management information systems (MIS) information also lacking.

Exhibit 6.2  STATE FLEET MANAGEMENT ACTIVITIES IN FOUR STATES[a]

|  | Ohio | New York | Michigan | Pennsylvania |
|---|---|---|---|---|
| **Type of Contract** |  |  |  |  |
| Competitive request for proposal | Yes | Yes | No | No |
| Pricing basis | Unit price | Unit price | Unit price | Unit price |
| Types of repairs covered | Preventive, routine | Preventive, routine, major | Preventive, routine | Preventive, routine, major |
| Number and type of vehicles covered | 3,000–3,500 passenger | 6,000 passenger | 3,500–3,700 passenger | 10,000–12,000 all types |
| Centralized/ decentralized | Decentralized | Centralized | Centralized | Decentralized |
| Vendor | Goodyear/ Goodrich | McCullagh Leasing | McCullagh Leasing | 400 vendors |
| Authorization required | $75 | $75 | $150 | $300/500 |
| Quality | Problems with all types | Better | About same | Better |
| Cost | Lower than if done individually | Lower (10–15% below Chilton) | About same | 10% lower than previous state operated |
| Management information system | Yes | Yes | Yes | Yes |
| Unique features | Some use of state-operated and corrections department facilities | One state-operated garage | Quasi-competition among dealers, state-operated garages, and contractor | Agreements with more than 400 vendors |

[a]These four states have agreements either with a single private vendor of with a number of vendors. The agreements list prices and location of maintenance facilities.

2. Types of repairs covered
   □ preventive,
   □ routine, and
   □ major.
3. Number and types of vehicles covered
   □ size of fleet and
   □ types of vehicles covered.
4. Central or decentralized ownership and responsibility for vehicles
   □ single central agency owning vehicles and
   □ individual agencies owning vehicles.

5. Number of vendors and locations
   □ single vendor,
   □ single vendor with multiple subcontracts,
   □ multiple vendors, and
   □ competition with state facilities.
6. Authorization for repairs
   □ level of threshold for repair authorization and
   □ management of authorization requests
7. Quality of service
   □ warranties for repairs,
   □ ease of access, and
   □ timeliness of repairs.
8. Costs
   □ economies of scale,
   □ discounts on repairs, and
   □ price comparisons.
9. Management information systems
   □ in-house and
   □ contracted.

A discussion of these issues in the four states follows. A summary of findings and recommendations on contracting follows the state examples.

**New York[3]**

*DESCRIPTION*

The State of New York has contracted for fleet maintenance since 1984. The central vehicle management division was given state-wide responsibility for vehicle maintenance in 1983. Maintenance had been the responsibility of the individual state agencies, but the state wanted to exercise more central control over these activities. During the 1970s, audits found instances of 400 percent markups on parts and $900–1,500 maintenance costs per vehicle per year. The state decided to try contracting because it had no idea how much was being spent on fleet maintenance and felt it had little control of maintenance activities. Approximately eight firms submitted proposals to the state when the initial request for proposals (RFP) was issued in 1983.

The current contractor is McCullagh Leasing, a national fleet maintenance firm. McCullagh does not actually do any of the maintenance; it subcontracts with a network of repair facilities throughout the state for all types of maintenance. The contract is for two years, with a state option to renew (up to two additional years). McCullagh receives price lists from its subcontractors annually. McCullagh's contract with the state guarantees prices, based on these price lists, on each maintenance activity, and includes warranties on all repairs performed. The contract prices apply to both years of the contract. Prices for renewal years include the percentage change in the Consumer Price Index for the preceding 12 months.

The contract covers preventive, routine, and major repairs for approximately 6,000 passenger vehicles and 15 passenger vans. The contract also covers emergency repairs and towing. Each vehicle operator has a special telephone number to call in case of emergency. Agencies are required to use either the contract repair facilities or state facilities (such as prison industry garages). Authorization from the state's fleet management office is required for repairs over $75. Operators have a toll-free 800 number to call for authorizations.

### ASSESSMENT

It took about two years for the agencies to adjust to the new arrangement. Some agencies initially refused to go to contract vendors, preferring instead to use vendors with which they were familiar. Displacement of state personnel was not a major problem because the few agencies that had their own garages were able to keep them if they wished.

The quality of service has not been actively monitored by the state (nor was it actively monitored before contracting began). The state believes that the warranties on repairs offer sufficient protection against poor service quality. A study done for the state in 1984 revealed that the state garage in Albany, which serves a 400-vehicle motor pool, processed 2.1 vehicles per day, considerably fewer than private firms. The state used this information to encourage the state repair facilities to become more competitive. Now they are more competitive, but the director of vehicle maintenance feels that their work is not of as high quality as the contractor's. The RFP stated that "periodic evaluations will be conducted by the state to assist in determining contractor performance adequacy," but no specific performance criteria were indicated in the RFP or contract.

Costs are 10–15 percent below *Chilton's* estimates for maintenance repairs.[4] The state cites economies of scale through one large negotiated contract and discounts on parts and repairs as the major reasons for the difference. The other important benefit is the state now has more centralized control over costs and can determine total expenditures for passenger vehicle maintenance.

### MIS

New York does not include all parts of its MIS within the contract. The contractor provides a computer tape of all repairs performed each month as the basis for billing. All other components are handled by state personnel. Each agency has a fleet coordinator. Every operator is required to fill out a monthly log documenting mileage, fuel costs, and maintenance costs. It is sent to the agency fleet coordinator, who then forwards it to the fleet management office. The state has developed computer software to track vehicle costs. Monthly, quarterly, and yearly reports are generated. The system provides information on the costs of maintenance for the life of each vehicle. Information is reported by agency and model of vehicle. The MIS does not track data on service quality, such as frequency of returns or the amount of time for repairs.

### Pennsylvania[5]

### DESCRIPTION

The State of Pennsylvania currently is using a quasi-contracting arrangement for its vehicle maintenance services through approximately 400 agreements with private vendors. These contract agreements specify the types of maintenance performed by the vendors, and the costs for each type. All three types of maintenance (preventive, routine, and major) are covered by the agreements, but any particular vendor may provide only certain services. Approximately 10,000–12,000 vehicles are maintained, including police vehicles and heavy duty trucks. The state supplies each vehicle operator with a book listing all vendors, their locations, hours of operation, the types of vehicles that each vendor repairs, and prices for maintenance services. The selection of a vendor is left to each operator, based on the least costly and most convenient alternative.

The state still operates one garage to handle some preventive and routine maintenance for a small pool of 150 vehicles. It is also used to handle overflow from private vendors. Operators use the state garage primarily when within 50 miles of Harrisburg. Outside this 50-mile radius, operators may use any private vendor listed. If operators are in an isolated area where access to listed vendors is not feasible, they may use the nearest service facility. Operators must request authorization for any repairs over $300 for passenger vehicles and over $500 for trucks from the state's automotive officer, who coordinates the repair information and cost estimate with the repair authorization section of the state garage.

The state has used these agreements since 1976, when it began to centralize some fleet maintenance and management activities. Previously, it operated three maintenance facilities (one each in the eastern, central, and western portions of the state). Operators found it inconvenient to use these facilities, particularly when operators were far from the facilities. In addition, the state believed that it could save money by using private vendors.

The agreement between the vendor and the state is for one year, with no option for renewal. Vendors include large garage chains and small independent garages and service stations. Each agreement specifies the hours of operation, types of maintenance work typically provided, labor rates, and information on discounts for parts.

Pennsylvania does not use a formal RFP process. Each year the state publishes an announcement soliciting information from interested vendors. Any vendor may be listed in the vendor book, but it is obligated to provide the listed services at the prices specified. Some agreements include provisions for emergency repairs or towing, but they vary by vendor. State vehicle operators are not required to use any particular listed vendor, and they are not constrained in the amount that they may spend with any single vendor.

ASSESSMENT

Pennsylvania has saved 10 percent of the cost of operating the three state facilities. The chief of the Vehicle Administration Division believes that it is mainly the discounts that account for the savings.

Repair quality is not formally monitored. The state assumes that operators will monitor quality on their own by not using vendors who provide poor service, but information about problems with particular vendors is not disseminated to other operators. Most operators are pleased with the convenience of this system, which the state believes has resulted in an overall increase in quality.

When the state made the transition to a private system, state employees in the closed facilities were absorbed within other agencies, transferred to the single remaining state garage, or terminated. The displacement of personnel was considered a minor problem because most were placed in other state government positions and the overall number of employees affected was small.

One problem with the system lies with the operators' discretion in selecting vendors. Although operators are supposed to select the most cost-effective vendor, there are no mechanisms to assure that they do, a situation that may result in the state's paying more than it should.

### MIS

The MIS function is handled in-house, using an IBM mainframe and personal computers to monitor vehicle maintenance and operation costs. Operators fill out monthly logs on vehicle usage for the data base on mileage, fuel costs, and maintenance costs. No information on service quality is collected.

### Ohio[6]

### DESCRIPTION

Ohio was among the first states to contract for fleet maintenance services. It contracts for fleet maintenance—but no other aspects of fleet management. Current contracts are with B. F. Goodrich and Goodyear, which bid jointly to provide preventive and routine maintenance for 3,000–3,500 passenger vehicles. Vehicles are purchased, owned, and managed by individual agencies. The two vendors provide prices to the state for all preventive and routine maintenance that is performed at their franchise outlets. The agencies take their vehicles to the vendors' outlets for service and are billed directly. Agencies are required to use the contract vendors, the state garage in Columbus, or prison repair facilities. Any repairs over $75 must be authorized by the fleet administrator's office. The fleet administrator serves as the central contract administrator and ensures that agencies receive the lowest possible cost by representing and negotiating for them as a group. Authorization allows the fleet administrator to note vehicles that have expensive repairs and to ensure adherence to the prices in the contract.

The contract does not cover major repairs. They are handled by private vendors who specialize in these kinds of repairs because most maintenance garages do not have the needed equipment or facilities. The state uses these vendors as any private individual would and has no specific contract with them. The state's maintenance contract covers towing, but not emergency service such as on-the-spot repairs or fuel. Only passenger vehicles are covered. State police, highway department, and other heavy vehicles are not included.

The contract is for one year with no provision for renewal. Only vendors registered with the state are eligible to bid. The contract is rebid annually, but B. F. Goodrich and Goodyear have held the contract for several years. Based on past expenditures, the contract specifies a $3.8 million total price, which is also the ceiling. Contractor selection is based on lowest price.

## ASSESSMENT

Ohio believes that there are unique problems with the quality of service provided by the private vendors as well as by state garages. Private contractors tend to try to "sell more than is needed" when doing repairs because most of their employees work on commission. Vendor contracts contains no provisions regarding quality of service. Most complaints about timeliness and quality are about repairs made in the state's prison industry garage.

The state has developed a system for channeling complaints through each state agency, then forwarding them to the state fleet administrator, who discusses the complaints with the contractor's representative. The state, however, does not keep formal records of complaints received.

The cost difference between the contract vendors and the state-operated facilities has not been systematically analyzed. The fleet administrator has documented instances in which repairs made by the state-operated garage cost more than contract vendor repairs. These discrepancies usually stem from work rules for state personnel that, for example, require two repairmen to tow a vehicle; the contractor sends only one to do the job. The fleet administrator believes that maintenance costs are lower than they would be if individual agencies contracted with vendors; the agencies' pooled efforts allow for economies of scale.

## MIS

The state is just beginning to implement an in-house MIS using an IBM mainframe and a software package, Mainstem, modified for its use. The MIS will allow the state to do life-cycle analysis of vehicle maintenance costs.

### Michigan[7]

#### DESCRIPTION

McCullagh Leasing has had an "agreement" with the State of Michigan since 1981 to provide preventive and routine maintenance for its passenger vehicle fleet. The state is uncomfortable calling this arrangement a contract because the agreement is simply a one-page pricing schedule set annually.

Michigan allows vehicle operators to use any of four options for maintenance of state vehicles: McCullagh, state-operated garages, authorized dealers (usually for repairs covered by the vehicle's original warranty), and local repair facilities. Operators are asked to use state-operated facilities primarily, using others when state-operated facilities are not available. All repairs exceeding $150 must be authorized by the state's mechanics. Approximately 30–35 percent of all maintenance is handled by the state-operated garages, the remainder by private vendors.

The state owns all vehicles and then leases them to its agencies at a rate that includes operating costs and overhead for the fleet management operation. The fleet is comprised of 3,500–3,700 passenger vehicles.

#### ASSESSMENT

Michigan decided to use private vendors to increase the options available to operators in locating convenient maintenance facilities. State facilities are limited in hours of operation, geographic distribution, and ability to handle the entire fleet.

State facilities are cost-competitive with the private vendors, but McCullagh's rates are lower than the other private vendors. Overall, the quality of vendor repairs is comparable to those in state-operated garages, but private vendors provide services in locations and at times that the state does not, such as evenings and weekends.

### MIS

Michigan uses an in-house MIS. The system software, called Cost and Management Maintenance System, is operated by three to four full-time staff. The majority of staff time is devoted to data entry and coding of information collected on vehicle operations and repair costs. Information is not collected on service quality.

---

## SUMMARY OF FINDINGS AND RECOMMENDATIONS ON GOVERNMENT PASSENGER FLEET MAINTENANCE CONTRACTING

States have approached contracting for vehicle maintenance in slightly different ways. Each of the four states covered here had somewhat different reasons for using the private sector.

### Scope of the Contract

Contracts range from one to four years (New York has a two-year contract with two renewal years). In part, shorter contracts are used to allow renegotiation of prices. Two states use competitive procurements for selecting a bidder and two do not. Each state uses unit prices as the basis for the cost of repairs. Only one specifies maximum expenditures in the contract, while the total cost is open ended in the others.

None of the four states uses performance or incentive contracts, but successful use of such contracts is possible. For example, Gainesville, Florida uses incentives for savings in total costs and in "rework" rates (i.e., the percentage of repairs that had to be redone) in its fleet maintenance contracts. The contractor receives 30 percent of any cost savings between the previous year's actual costs and the target cost set in the contract for the current year, but it is also penalized 30 percent for any costs over the target. The contractor also receives a quality incentive bonus for a rework rate below 5 percent.

**Types of Repairs Covered**

Two states contract only for preventive and routine maintenance, and two contract for major repairs as well. Interestingly, the two states contracting only for preventive and routine maintenance were also the two that felt their costs were lower when they switched to contracting. Although available data currently do not permit determining whether costs are lower only for certain types of repairs, the states should investigate the possibility of contracting only for repairs that offer significant cost savings.

**Number and Types of Vehicles Covered**

The number of vehicles covered by contracts in the four states varied from 3,000 to 12,000. A higher number of vehicles covered may lead to economies of scale. It is also possible that contracting is efficient only for certain types of vehicles. The states should monitor maintenance costs for different types (e.g., models, sizes) of passenger vehicles.

**Centralized or Decentralized Ownership and Responsibility for Vehicles**

Two of the states have central ownership and responsibility for vehicles and two have decentralized systems. Centralized administration may allow for more thorough monitoring of costs under contracting. Centralized administration also may make it easier to begin contracting because mechanisms exist that tie agency fleets together, allowing them to negotiate as a single unit.

**Number of Vendors and Locations**

There are tradeoffs in using one versus multiple-contract vendors. Even when a single contractor has multiple locations, it can probably provide more consistent service than several vendors by offering consistent pricing and warranties. The disadvantage of a single vendor is that it may be less motivated to offer competitive prices in parts of the state where, for example, labor costs, are much lower. Multiple contracts allow a state to access more facilities, but it may sacrifice the guaranteed pricing and warranties of a single vendor, making cost monitoring more difficult. Using multiple contractors also creates potential problems in implementing an MIS—

they would provide information that could be more easily entered into a data base had one contractor been the source.

Another option is using private vendors without contracts. This arrangement provides the most location options, but effectively eliminates control over prices and warranties. Further, state personnel are more likely to use the most convenient location regardless of price, so costs are likely to be higher.

Another important consideration is whether the state should continue to maintain its own garages in competition with the contractor; doing so may encourage competition, thus lowering costs to the state. It may be necessary when the vendor cannot handle all vehicles or types of repairs or when the state needs to maintain a small centralized motor pool.

### Authorization for Repairs

All four states require authorization for repairs above a certain dollar amount. This provision gives the state a chance to evaluate potentially unreasonable costs before repairs are made. The maximum should be set at a level that allows the state to monitor major expenditures but not to be swamped and therefore delay authorization requests. The experience of these four states and that of several others suggests that a $150 limit balances these factors.

### Quality of Service

None of the four states monitored the quality of repairs. They seemed to feel that repair warranties were sufficient protection from poor service. They also felt that the service provided by contractors was equal to or better than that of state garages. Timeliness of repairs and accessibility should also be considered in measuring the quality of service. Contractors may offer lower prices, but if repairs are not timely or if significant time is required to access the contractor's facilities, these considerations may outweigh the cost savings.

Exhibit 6.3 suggests criteria for assessing service quality. Without performance standards based on systematically collected information on the quality of repairs, it is virtually impossible to evaluate service from different providers. Information must be collected on the quality of repairs, both by state garages and private vendors, so that performance standards can be developed to protect the state from poor service. Performance standards should be used to ensure

Exhibit 6.3  SERVICE QUALITY CRITERIA FOR ASSESSING FLEET
           MAINTENANCE

---

1. *Safety.* This criterion is probably the number one concern—that vehicles be kept in a condition that is safe for drivers and passengers (i.e., accidents relating to defective vehicle condition should be kept at a minimum).

2. *Turnaround time for repairs.* This criterion is a major indicator of the timeliness of the work done.

3. *Return rates* (i.e., percentage of repairs that must be returned because the work done was not correct or complete). This criterion is a major indicator of the quality of the work.

4. *Number of vehicle breakdowns while on the road.* This criterion is also an important indicator of maintenance quality—both of preventive maintenance and of repairs.

5. *Average client travel time to and from the maintenance facilities.* This is a major indicator of the convenience of the option. The travel time for government employees should be a major consideration; travel time to get vehicle maintenance can become a substantial cost. Distances from clients to maintenance facilities can be used as a proxy for travel time if necessary. For example, an option that provides vendor pickup and delivery of vehicles would be very attractive on this criterion. (However, such an arrangement could involve extra cost to the organization that did the pickup and delivery. This cost probably would be passed on in some form to the state. It should be considered in the cost analysis.)

6. *Client waiting time.* Vehicles that are not ready when promised or prolonged time to collect vehicles, causing government employees to have to wait at the facility, can be a significant problem, especially when pickups are done during working hours. Similarly, long waits at the facility to check vehicles in can be a major problem.

7. *Hours of operation.* Facilities that allow pickup and delivery of vehicles over longer hours (e.g., early, late, weekends) will be more convenient for at least some clients.

8. *Quality of amenities.* Amenities include the physical attractiveness of the maintenance facilities and their surroundings, the attractiveness of waiting areas, and the courteousness of employees. For example, facilities located in areas that are perceived to be dangerous will be resisted by clients.

9. *Ability to respond to emergencies.* Options that provide quick response when needed are preferable. However, emergency towing service could be handled as a separate activity, provided by state employees or under contract, regardless of the arrangement the state makes for maintenance.

10. *Staying power/consequences of interruption.* What is the likelihood of an unexpected interruption of service because of labor problems such as strikes and slowdowns or to financial problems such as cuts in funding or bankruptcy? How frequently are expected interruptions of service likely to occur, such as those due to normal rebidding of contracts? To what extent are such interruptions likely to cause problems for the agency? Is the option reversible once it is in place—if there is a need to switch back?

11. *Ability to:* (1) *meet changing state needs, such as those due to changes in vehicle characteristics or operating conditions and* (2) *take advantage of the latest developments in the technology of service delivery.* Will some options be

Exhibit 6.3 *Continued*

more flexible amid such changes and, thus, provide a higher-quality service to the state in the future?

12. *Accountability of the operation.* To what extent can performance of the service provider be monitored and controlled to meet the needs of the state agencies using the service? For example, an agency may have closer control over its own personnel, or state agencies may find it easier to establish formal procedures to monitor contractors' performance and hold them accountable than to monitor programs delivered by their own employees.

Source: The Urban Institute and The Council of State Governments, "State of Delaware Recommended Process for Analysis of Service Delivery Alternatives," July 1987.

that contractors maintain an acceptable level of performance on timeliness of repairs, return rates, client waiting time, and other factors. This information indicates the performance of both public and private providers, and the states can then take necessary steps to maintain service quality. This information should be included in the MIS.

Word-of-mouth as a method of identifying vendors who are performing poorly does not work. An affected state employee may not return to an offending vendor, but the message of poor service is unlikely to reach other state agencies or even other vehicle operators in the same agency. Some formal centralized tracking is needed. At the least, it should take the form of a formal complaint process, with complaints tabulated regularly by vendor and disseminated frequently. Preferably, a short questionnaire could be sent to vehicle operators asking about their levels of satisfaction on such criteria as those shown in exhibit 6.3.

### Costs

Costs are a major consideration in switching to, and subsequently evaluating, contracting. Cost savings are often the primary motivating force. Contracting offers savings through economies of scale when a contract covers a sufficient number of agencies or vehicles. Contracting may also be a mechanism for price discounts from vendors interested in establishing a consistent source of business. States should be careful to make cost comparisons only for comparable repairs.

Any process that encourages competition is likely to result in cost savings. Competitive RFP procedures encourage vendors to reduce costs. When state-operated garages provide price lists and these lists and contracted vendor prices are disseminated, the resulting competition could motivate public garages to increase efficiency. Mechanisms should be implemented to encourage operators to use the least costly alternative when competition exists between public and private facilities or among contract vendors. Providing incentives or requirements to use the least costly alternative helps ensure reduced costs and spur greater competition among providers.

### Management Information Systems

None of the states we surveyed contracted for an MIS as part of its fleet maintenance contract, through Delaware seriously considered it. At least one vendor submitted data to the state on vehicle maintenance costs. The states should consider including this service in their fleet maintenance contracts. Keeping MIS in-house allows the state to oversee information quality and make changes when problems arise. Depending on a contractor for this service may mean surrendering oversight of data collection, offering potential for error. When this function is contracted, the state must ensure its easy transferability to a new contractor.

In either case, the MIS is extremely important. It provides vital information for tracking maintenance costs on individual vehicles that is needed to determine optional replacement timing and types and models of vehicles with good maintenance cost histories. Without such a system, it is virtually impossible to assess the cost and quality of services, in-house or contracted. Effective administration of fleet maintenance services requires that managers have access to and use this information. Unless such a system exits, evaluating quality and costs of fleet maintenance contracting alternatives is essentially intuitive.

---

### CONCLUSION

Contracting for vehicle maintenance enables state governments to improve quality and lessen costs. The issues discussed above should be considered by states in electing whether to contract and in selecting the specific arrangement. Upon careful assessment, states can select options to fit their particular needs and objectives.

Although contracting for fleet maintenance and management has been the primary service delivery alternative used by states, there are other possibilities. Instead of retaining its passenger vehicle fleet, states could lease vehicle fleets including maintenance, as many large corporations do. Another alternative is to issue vouchers to state employees for fuel and maintenance costs in return for using their own vehicles for state business. The states could also investigate a public-private partnership with a large private firm or utility that maintains a passenger fleet of its own and share facilities and costs.

Regardless of the alternatives considered, adequate information is imperative. Without information on current costs and quality of fleet maintenance services, assessing alternatives is severely limited.

---

## Notes

1. Telephone survey conducted by the Council of State Governments and detailed interviews conducted by The Urban Institute during March and April 1987.

2. The author would like to thank Kenneth Voytek, formerly with The Urban Institute, for his contribution to this chapter. Mr. Voytek conducted the initial interviews with the states described and reviewed the chapter for accuracy.

3. Telephone interview with James Willette, Chief, New York Vehicle Administrative Services, and Thomas Kieper, Director of Statewide Vehicle Maintenance, March 1987.

4. Chilton publishes lists of the typical costs and time involved in making a range of repairs for all vehicles. *Chilton's Auto Service Manual* and *Chilton's Labor Guide and Parts Manual*, Motor Age Professional Mechanic's ed. (Radner, Pa.: Chilton Book Company, 1987).

5. This section is based on a telephone interview with Robert Kitsock, Chief, Vehicle Administration Division, Pennsylvania Bureau of Vehicle Management, April 1987.

6. This section is based on a telephone interview with Ronald Remey, Ohio Fleet Administrator, March 1987.

7. This section is based on a telephone interview with Kathy Rushford Carter, Director, Michigan Motor Transportation Division, March 1987.

# Chapter Seven

# USE OF THE PRIVATE SECTOR FOR STATE TRANSPORTATION ACTIVITIES

*Joan W. Allen*

Opportunities for the private sector to assist in carrying out some state transportation responsibilities include but are not limited to:

☐ road and bridge construction;
☐ road and bridge maintenance and repair (including rest areas);
☐ issuance of driver's and motor vehicle license renewals; and
☐ operation of state toll bridges, toll roads, and ferries.

For many years, states contracted for road construction and major reconstruction; they are not discussed here. This chapter focuses on the use of contractors for road and bridge maintenance and repairs and the use of the private sector for help issuing driver's and motor vehicle licenses. In addition, operation of toll facilities is briefly discussed. (States are also often responsible for special transportation assistance in rural areas and for the elderly. The private sector is often used for this type of assistance.[1])

## CONTRACTING FOR STATE ROAD MAINTENANCE AND REPAIR

The following definitions are useful in a discussion of road maintenance and repair:

Reconstruction [is] rebuilding an existing road or bridge. Repair projects provide better mobility on roadways and for increased volume or load capacity. Road maintenance represents a conglomerate of many different work activities that are necessary to preserve the facilities in a safe, efficient and usable condition.

Maintenance is usually classified as either routine or periodic. Routine maintenance includes activities that normally are repeated during the year. Periodic maintenance includes operations that need to be repeated only as necessary over the years.[2]

As noted above, the states generally contract for major construction and reconstruction of roads and bridges. The concern here is contracting for road and bridge repaving and other maintenance and repair activities. Exhibit 7.1 summarizes the road *maintenance* contracting practices of the 50 states (including repaving but not major reconstruction). The list indicates that contracting for at least some maintenance and repair is fairly common, but what is covered is not always clear.

In the following sections, we discuss contracting for road and bridge repair and maintenance in: California, Illinois, Iowa, and Pennsylvania. Special contracts in the District of Columbia are also discussed.

### California[3]

#### DESCRIPTION

In California, state employees do approximately 90 percent of repaving and other maintenance of state roads, guardrails, highway fences, and similar structures; the remainder is contracted for. The contracts total approximately $50 million a year, 70–80 percent of it for repaving.

California contracts for some work partly from precedent and partly from the shortage of state personnel. As a state official commented, "Sometimes it's easier to get people, sometimes money" in the budget process.

California has a long precedent of contracting for some repaving. In contrast, maintaining roadside rest areas has been contracted for only three or four years. This work is now entirely contracted for because of the state's successful contracting experience and the difficulty in obtaining approval for additional state employees.

Contractor employees have not replaced state employees for California road work, but the state hires fewer workers than it would were less work contracted for.

Contracts for road repairs are of two types: *project* contracts in which the contractor is responsible for repaving or other repair for a given segment of road, with a time limit for completion of the work, and *activity* contracts for general activities such as roadside

Exhibit 7.1  EXTENT OF CONTRACTING FOR STATE ROAD MAINTENANCE AND REPAIR (excluding new construction)

| State | Repair | Maintenance (patching and sealing) |
|---|---|---|
| Alabama | None | None |
| Alaska | 85–92% contracted | None |
| Arizona | Jobs over $50,000 | Pavement sealing |
| Arkansas | Most reconstruction | Very little |
| California | Unknown | Unknown |
| Colorado | None | Some patching and bridge deck repairs |
| Connecticut | Most | Most |
| Delaware | Most | Most except winter maintenance |
| Florida | All | All except signs |
| Georgia | All | None |
| Hawaii | About 70% | 90% of state work |
| Idaho | Some | Some |
| Illinois | Unknown | None except some signs |
| Indiana | Jobs over $100,000 | Most |
| Iowa | Some | Some |
| Kansas | All | Some |
| Kentucky | All | None |
| Louisiana | Jobs over $30,000 | None |
| Maine | Unknown | 50% |
| Maryland | Unknown | Most |
| Massachusetts | Unknown | Some |
| Michigan | Unknown | Very little |
| Minnesota | Unknown | Most |
| Mississippi | Jobs over $200,000 | Little |
| Missouri | Most | If biddable competitively |
| Montana | Unknown | None |
| Nebraska | Most | Some, such as joint and crack sealing |
| Nevada | Some | Some |
| New Hampshire | All | None under $10,000 |
| New Jersey | Some—increasing | Some—increasing |
| New Mexico | Some | Some |
| New York | Unknown | Some |
| North Carolina | All | Little |
| North Dakota | Some | None |
| Ohio | Jobs over $10,000/mile and $20,000/bridge | Jobs over $10,000/mile and $20,000/bridge |
| Oklahoma | 50–60% resurfacing, paving | Most |
| Oregon | Some | Some |
| Pennsylvania | Most | Most |
| Rhode Island | Some | Very little |
| South Carolina | Some | Some |
| South Dakota | Unknown | Very little |

Exhibit 7.1 *Continued*

| State | Repair | Maintenance (patching and sealing) |
|---|---|---|
| Tennessee | Unknown | Department of Transportation planning on increasing contracting to 50% of work |
| Texas | Most | Most |
| Utah | Unknown | Some—increasing |
| Vermont | Jobs over $40,000 | Unknown |
| Virginia | Some—increasing | Some |
| Washington | Jobs over $25,000 | Very little |
| West Virginia | Jobs over $25,000 | Unknown |
| Wisconsin | Unknown | Unknown |
| Wyoming | Jobs over $25,000 | Some |

Source: Based on Cheryl O. Ronk, "A Look at Using Contractors and Government Employees on Public Work Projects," Michigan Road Builders Association, 1986. It was based on a 1984 mail survey of all 50 states. Some states also contract for weed and grass cutting, litter collection, and landscape and rest room maintenance. Some farmers are paid for roadside mowing, which contractors tend to find unprofitable.

"Unknown" indicates that the source material did not provide sufficient information to make a determination.

rest area maintenance. Project contracts specify a guaranteed price. Activity contracts specify a maximum number of hours of work; they have ceilings but not floors. The bidder whose reasonable *estimate* on materials and labor is lowest is awarded the contract but is paid according to actual personnel and equipment costs, calculated after the job is completed.

The state usually has no trouble locating enough bidders to make the contracting process competitive. If there are not enough bidders for a contract of if bids seem too high, the state readvertises and encourages additional bids.

California road repair contracts range from $1,000 to $4 million or $5 million. They include late penalties, but probably only 2–3 percent of contractors incur such penalties. Contracts do not include bonuses for completing jobs ahead of schedule.

A state employee, called a resident engineer, is on site most of the time for most repairs. The engineer tests materials, such as oil temperature, and monitors various procedures. Other inspectors sometimes help with testing on a big job. Activity contracts, such as for roadside rest area maintenance, are monitored daily or weekly.

The state has considered contracting for complete maintenance of particular road segments over a period of a year or so, but its constitution does not allow this type of contract. State employee groups support this restriction.

## ASSESSMENT

The state has not directly compared the costs or quality of contracted maintenance work with that done by state employees. A California official reports that it is difficult to compare contracted jobs for quality and cost because of the many variables—the condition of the pavement or guardrail when it requires repair and the weather conditions when the job has to be done, for example. State inspectors prepare an evaluation form after each job, but not much use is made of it. If the contractor's work is judged unsatisfactory initially, it must be completed satisfactorily before the state pays for the work. Both contractors and state employees generally complete their jobs on time, satisfactorily, and at anticipated costs. Neither quality nor cost of work differs significantly regardless of who does the work.

A lengthy bidding process is the principle drawback to contracting for road repair in California. But an emergency procedure enables the state to act within a day to contract for work to correct hazardous conditions.

California officials believe that the state contracting act, which specifies what one official described as a "rigid, inflexible process," ensures honesty and quality on all sides. They recommend such legislation to other states that may not have such secure controls over contracting.

## DAVIS-BACON PROVISIONS

A California official has a complaint that applies to contracting in all states. He believes that the federal Davis-Bacon Act is not in the public interest. It dictates that workers on jobs for which any federal funds are used must be paid at least the "prevailing wage" for their type of work in the area where their jobs are. In spite of recent relaxation of some requirements of the law, it still costs California citizens millions of dollars. Other state and local officials agree.

**Illinois[4]**

*DESCRIPTION*

The State of Illinois contracts for approximately 20 percent of its road maintenance, including patching, pavement repair, guardrail and fence repairs, seal coating, bridge deck patching, and other miscellaneous jobs. Of the total $180 million budgeted for state road maintenance, Illinois contracts for about $35–40 million. Most contracts are short term, ranging from two weeks to a few months, and are for a specific job.

The Maintenance Division expanded its contracting about 20 percent in 1983, when it received $20 million additional funds because of an increase in the gas tax. The agency expects to expand contracting further when more funds become available. The state increased contracting partly because it was not possible to get approval for additional state employees to do the work. No state maintenance employees have been added in the past few years. Another reason for contracting was objections by outside trade unions when state employees were used for such duties as guardrail repair. A metal trades union complained that members of the Teamsters (the state employee union) could not do metal work.

Inspectors in each of the nine regional offices monitor the work of contract, city, and state employees. Major jobs that are contracted for are monitored daily on site, as is the practice in most states.

*ASSESSMENT*

Illinois has not made any explicit comparisons between the costs of contracted work and similar work done by state employees. The state official interviewed believes that Illinois is saving overhead costs (e.g., office rental) by contracting with cities for maintenance work and is saving on the cost and depreciation of heavy equipment by using contractors.

The major problems are with relatively small contractors that cannot do the work they think they can. Stricter prequalification procedures may eliminate some of this problem.

The state asked the Federal Highway Administration (FHWA) in 1986 to do a "process review" of inspections of contracted jobs throughout the state because the maintenance department was concerned about the quality of some contract work. When the FHWA visited 15–20 sites, it found that some inspections of relatively small jobs were being done by inspectors who were not sufficiently qualified. As a result of the review process, the state has made changes in its specifications and monitoring procedures in the areas of bridge painting, pavement patching and guard rail maintenance.

## Iowa

### DESCRIPTION

The State of Iowa contracts for road and bridge work such as bridge painting, spot leveling, pavement repair, and crack and joint repair. The budget for work by public employees is about $76 million, for contracts, $12 million. Thus, approximately 14 percent of road and bridge maintenance and repair that is not major reconstruction is contracted for.[5]

The state uses public employees as jacks of all trades in road and bridge maintenance. The jobs that require the greatest skill and the most sophisticated equipment are contracted for and have been for many years. For example, Iowa judges it more efficient to contract for the complete repainting of a bridge than to have state employees spot paint as the need arises. If state employees were used for the complete repainting job, too many would be drawn off other necessary maintenance. The same situation is true for spot leveling, especially for large areas of road.

Contracts are generally for 30 days or less. They are awarded on the basis of low bid. The state receives anywhere from 1 to 10 or 15 bids on contracts. There are few bidders for small contracts in rural areas (e.g., a $3,500 contract for delivery of 100 tons of aggregate from the only rock quarry near a road project). The state is satisfied with the number of bidders except in rural areas, where there is no apparent remedy to the scarcity of contractors for small jobs. Contracts may run as low as $3,000 or as high as $500,000, such as one for large areas of pavement repair and bridge painting.[6]

Penalties are written into contracts for time overruns. Unsatisfactory work must be remedied by the contractor before payment. The state is presently considering whether to award bonuses for completion of work ahead of schedule.

An inspector is assigned to each contracted job and is on site most of the time. The inspector has a copy of both the contract and specifications. When a job is completed, the inspector fills out an evaluation form, which is filed centrally and becomes part of the contract record. When problems with a contractor arise, the inspector and resident engineer try to work with the contractor to improve performance. If performance does not improve, the contractor's future bids may not be accepted.

For the 18 months from January 1982 to 30 June 1983, the Department of Transportation experimented with *general contracts*, contracts covering a large number of road maintenance services over an extended period—rather than contracts for specific jobs and over shorter periods. The contracts included as many as 22 tasks. The state accepted bids and then contracted with four companies, each for road maintenance in a different region. The contracts ranged from $247,911 to $664,160.[7] (The States of South Dakota and Florida also experimented with contracts under which the contractors do all maintenance for segments of road over an extended period.[8] In both states, contractors had difficulty bidding because they could not figure out the quantities of materials needed for a necessarily unspecified number of jobs.)[9]

### ASSESSMENT

The Iowa Senate required an evaluation of the feasibility of general contracting. The Highway Department compared performance and costs for several contractors, each doing *all* maintenance on 69–100 miles of state roads, with those of state employees doing the same work on comparable stretches.

On average, the work done by contractors cost approximately 67 percent more than that done by state employees. Contractor costs for maintenance were 151–186 percent of the cost for which state employees could have performed identical tasks.[10]

State officials believe that the higher costs were probably due to contractor unfamiliarity with some of the work, higher labor costs for the contractors, profit, and interest that the contractors had to pay on borrowed capital. Mowing shoulders and medians, burn/plane surfacing, and sweeping showed the largest differences in costs. Unit costs for spall patching, shoulder repair with aggregates, rebuilding shoulders with earth, bridge painting, and like tasks were about the same for contractors and state employees.[11]

The state listed the following recurring problems with contractors in each of its four districts:

☐ lack of necessary equipment when needed,
☐ failure of contractor to understand work descriptions,

☐ lack of experienced/qualified personnel to perform some functions,
☐ poor work,
☐ tardiness,
☐ distance of bases of operation from maintenance areas,
☐ poor communication between contractor and workers,
☐ failure of workers to use safety equipment and proper traffic control, and
☐ insufficient contact between contractor and adjacent property owners.[12]

The state report on the experiment concluded that general contracting (involving many services) should not be pursued further but that functional contracting should be used when contractors are able to achieve competitive unit costs, such as for spall patching, joint and crack filling, full depth patching, aggregate shoulder repair, seal coating, and bridge painting.[13]

Additional considerations in decisions on whether to contract for certain functions are limited state personnel and the cost of sophisticated equipment. The state continues to contract for the most technologically demanding work, and state employees do the jobs that require less technical skills.

In general, state officials do not have many problems with contracting for road repair because they are "selective on what we contract." They have had no complaints from worker unions on contracting. The state believes that the capacity to contract for some jobs gives it greater flexibility to complete big jobs and would like to contract for more jobs because there is "much more work necessary than we are able to do [with limited staff and money]."

The work of contractors is generally "very satisfactory," and Iowa has increased its contracting at least 10 percent in the last 10 years. It gives particular credit for contracting success to the practice of holding a preconstruction conference among the contractor, the resident engineer for the project, and the state inspector assigned to the project. The conference allows participants to discuss any major issues relative to a project before work begins.

**Pennsylvania**

*DESCRIPTION*

The Commonwealth of Pennsylvania contracts for about 50 percent of tar and chip roadway surface treatment, 50–80 percent of paving (depending on the geographical region), at least 95 percent of road-side insecticide spraying, and about 95 percent of bridge maintenance, including painting.[14]

Contracting is done at the maintenance district level. (Maintenance districts usually follow county lines.) The number of maintenance personnel authorized in state budgets has been cut over the past few years; state personnel formerly did most road maintenance work. Regions now usually prefer contracting for "extensive" paving jobs so that the pool of state employees is not seriously depleted for one job. In addition, Pennsylvania tends to contract work that necessitates costly heavy equipment.

The two major reasons given by Pennsylvania officials for contracting are a lack of state employees and the contractors' expertise, particularly for extensive paving.[15]

Road maintenance and repair contracts are usually project specific. Exceptions are contracts for herbicide spraying, which may be written for a year or so, and guardrail repair contracts, which specify that the contractor shall work when called by the state.

Rest area maintenance and operation contracts are written for one year. They specify the rate paid for a certain number of hours to be spent for plumbing, electrical work, carpentry, and painting, and they also specify lump sum payments for cleaning and operation of the rest areas and of wastewater and drinking water facilities. A fiscal year 1988 contract for two Pennsylvania rest areas combined totaled $71,100.[16]

Contracting is usually competitive. When bids are scarce, the state regional managers ask nonbidders why they did not participate in order to discover any difficulties with the work description or the process. Bidders submit their proposed costs per hour or per activity.

Regional or state inspectors monitor the work. On large contracts, records are kept in case they are needed later should work prove defective.

ASSESSMENT

A consulting firm managed a demonstration project comparing the work of a contractor and state employees between mid-October 1980 and 30 June 1981. Their tasks were similar, including snow removal and other winter maintenance and some summer maintenance on 309 miles of highway (contractor responsibility) and another 291 miles of highway (state employee responsibility) in Clearfield County.[17]

As a result of the study, state transportation officials decided that one contract in Clearfield County should cover grading unpaved shoulders, cleaning ditches, and replacing pipe and that unpaved road maintenance, mechanized patching, and surface treatment should continue to be contracted for separately. State employees would be responsible for base repair, stabilizing unpaved shoulders, sweeping, and special projects.[18] The consultants noted that maintenance and repair work could be accomplished by fewer staff than the state was then using. They also recommended developing contract documents around maintenance activity standards rather than construction work specifications.[19] There are other consultant recommendations that any state can apply:[20]

☐ Potential bidders should be given the option of one-, two- or three-year bids.

☐ Radios should be required and included in the bid price to improve rapid communication.

☐ Bidding with combinations of department-supplied cutting edges for plows, plows and plow frames, and sanders should be tested across the state.

☐ Follow-up sessions should be conducted with contractors from the previous winter operations to identify and solve problems.

☐ Training should be provided to potential new contractors in how to plow and sand and how to set up equipment for performance and safety.

☐ Information should be circulated early regarding bid dates.

☐ Prebid conferences should be conducted to answer questions and provide contract preparation assistance.

The consultants also recommended that Department of Transportation personnel work with successful bidders to help them develop expertise in performing maintenance work and to ensure that they will continue to bid on maintenance work.[21]

The consultants worked out unit costs for contractors and for state employees for 38 work activities. The consultants estimated that a 12 percent reduction in state personnel with contracting would produce a cost savings of 4.8 percent, a 64 percent reduction would save the state 5.6 percent of its unit costs, and contracting *all* state road maintenance and repair would save the government 10.6 percent.[22]

The study described above included cost comparisons and indicated what work was best contracted for and what should be done by state employees.

State officials rated the work of contractors generally satisfactory on timeliness and durability. They plan to continue contracting at about the present rate.

### District of Columbia[23]

*DESCRIPTION*

The District of Columbia (D.C.) contracts for approximately 61 percent of the maintenance and repairs done on its roads. In 1967, the street maintenance division employed 350 people for this work; current employment is 115, or approximately 33 percent of the former work force.

Public employees do all pothole patching in the District, 99 percent of bridge maintenance, and some other minor repairs. The remaining work is done through two types of contracts: those for approximately 60 days, for specific jobs in joint sealing and slurry sealing, and contracts for six to eight months for all asphalt repair and all repair of concrete roadways, sidewalks, and alleys. Four contracts are awarded for the asphalt and concrete activities, for a total of about $4 million a year.

The asphalt and concrete work contracts are bid on the basis of estimated materials and labor and are paid on actual costs of materials and labor. The shorter specific-project contracts are based on unit price per square foot of work.

When D.C. roads officials made cost comparisons more than 30 years ago, they decided to increase contracting gradually; they had neither the work force nor the equipment for major jobs. The long-term contracts for all asphalt and concrete repair have been bid for at least 30 years. Until about four years ago, joint sealing was done by public employees, but an informal cost comparison convinced officials to begin contracting for the work.

*ASSESSMENT*

D.C. officials are equally satisfied with the work of its contractors and its public employees, although they say that the quality of both has deteriorated over the years. They find contracting all asphalt work and all concrete work to four contractors a satisfactory way to get the work done.

**British Columbia Emerging Effort[24]**

The Canadian Province of British Columbia has begun a major experiment to restructure the delivery of maintenance of provincial roads and bridges. (Canadian provinces are similar to our states.)

The province has decided to switch to contracting for its road and bridge maintenance services—about $450 million worth of these services. The Ministry of Transportation and Highways has divided the province into 28 contract areas. For each a competition is being held. The winning contractors are being given three-year contracts. The province is selling small assets such as light equipment to the contractor and is leasing them facilities and heavy equipment. The contractors are responsible for all road and bridge maintenance in the contract area.

A notable aspect of the British Columbia effort is its attempt to give its current employees first preference for the contracts. Any bid from an employee group will be given a "five percent preference" over nonemployee groups. As of September 1988, 18 of the 28 competitions had been completed. Employee groups were successful bidders in seven areas and private sector bidders in the other eleven. Each new employer agreed to accept the government employees union as bargaining agent. All 1,355 of the affected employees are being offered work by the new companies with the same pay and benefits.

Implementation of this effort is just beginning—with the first contract (covering the Southern Vancouver Island area) effective 1 September 1988. Thus, we are unable to provide any after-the-fact evaluation information. This first contract is priced at $29.9 million over the three-year contract team, which the province reports is $1.1 million less than projected ministry costs.

**Summary of Findings and Recommendations on Contracting for Road Maintenance and Repair**

The practice of contracting for a portion of road and bridge maintenance and repairs is well-established in many states.[25] The four states we reviewed were generally satisfied with contract work and planned to continue contracting. Supervision by field engineers seems to encourage contractors to do quality work. Costs for some major types of work are comparable to or are lower than those for work by state employees. It appears that contracting for substantial amounts of road maintenance and repair is appropriate and that it should continue, with state employees used primarily for less-specialized and less-skilled jobs. However, the 18-month Iowa study showed that contracting for some but not all maintenance and repair activities is efficient.

Almost all state contracting is on a per-project basis. Iowa, South Dakota, and Florida experimented with contracts whereby the contractor maintains a segment of road over an extended period (e.g., one year) and covers a defined list of activities instead of specific jobs. For this type of contract, contractors are asked to bid an *estimated* number of units of materials and labor but are paid *actual* costs. Sometimes costs are more than the bid, sometimes less.[26] One option is fixed-price bids on specific lengths of road to be maintained.

Iowa contractors could not compete with state personnel on a cost basis for many activities. The state, therefore, recommended the use of contractors whose costs are competitive. South Dakota and Florida noted contractor difficulty estimating materials needed for an unspecified number of jobs. States commonly have seasonal, six-month, or annual contracts for such jobs as pothole patching and guardrail repair for a given road segment, for which the costs are more easily estimated.[27]

As the Iowa evaluation indicates, vendors' unfamiliarity with some of the work can be a problem. We suggest that states experiment with giving contractors responsibility for specific road segments for, say, a year; the contracts would be for specific maintenance and repair activities that the contractors appear to be able to handle at a cost comparable to that of state employees'. The Michigan Road Builders Association reports that several states are considering contracts for relatively long periods whereby contractors are responsible for specific tasks along given segments of road (e.g., pothole patching or guardrail repair), for which the contractors would receive set annual fees.[28]

An even greater departure from current practice that states might consider is to hold district competitions for road and bridge maintenance and repair work in which state employees vie with private contractors for certain projects. An independent financial/audit agency would review all bids and decide the winners. (This plan is the Phoenix model that the Phoenix Department of Public Works uses, apparently with considerable success.)

We recommend that states compare the performance of contractors and state employees on particular functions to identify activities that are best done by one group or the other.

## USE OF THE PRIVATE SECTOR FOR RENEWAL OF DRIVER'S AND MOTOR VEHICLE LICENSES

The experiences of Florida, Minnesota, and New Jersey, which have used the private sector in issuing driver's and motor vehicle licenses, are discussed below.

### Florida

#### DESCRIPTION[29]

In 1985, Florida began a pilot program in which retail stores provide space and pay for utilities and maintenance of "offices" where state employees issue driver's license renewals and duplicates. Two Eckerd Drug Company stores in Pinellas County and a table supply retail store in Broward County provide the space.

The principal reason the state tried this approach was the growing number of complaints about crowded state offices and long waits for service. The pilot offices, located in shopping malls, offer added convenience to the public. They have longer and more flexible hours: 9:30 a.m. to 7:30 p.m., six days a week. Large regular state driver's license offices are open from 7 a.m. to 6 p.m. five days a week, but the smaller ones are open those hours only four days a week.

The benefits to private businesses that donate space include good public relations and the possibility of additional business from license applicants.

Approximately 8 percent of the licenses issued in one region and 3 percent in the other were issued through the private outlets in 1986. Each region has nine driver's license offices, including those in stores. Because the state pays no rent or utilities for space in these stores, it thinks that it saves money by using the stores instead of adding more regular offices. A regional administrator inspects all driver's license outlets two or three times a month.

The Driver's License Bureau has not attempted to increase the number of store outlets, primarily because money has not been budgeted for the expensive cameras that additional offices need.

#### ASSESSMENT

Florida Driver's License Bureau officials are fully satisfied with the pilot program.[30] A study done by the Florida Department of Highway Safety and Motor Vehicles after the retail store space had been used for approximately a year, however, concluded that the productivity at the three sites did not justify the costs but "what may be important here is that the clientele perceive they are benefitting and that, in itself, may be worth the premium paid and may serve to support continuation of the program in the future in highly populated areas."[31]

The department did a mail survey of individuals renewing at express (retail) and regular driver's license offices between September 1985 and May 1986. The average waiting time in retail stores was three minutes, compared to eleven minutes for state offices. Service was rated "very good" by 87 percent of the clientele at retail offices but by only 57 percent at regular state offices. An additional 31 percent of the latter rated service at the regular offices "good," as did an additional 9 percent at express offices.

The study also examined office productivity. The two express renewal offices in drug stores in Pinellas County did 4.5 percent of the driver's license business there for 6.1 percent of the cost. The office in the store in Broward County did 1.8 percent of the business for 2.2 percent of the cost. The state calculated that "to reach workload/cost parity would require an increase in applicants of 35.7 percent and 24.9 percent for [the retail offices in] Pinellas and Broward Counties respectively," but the authors of the study did not think it would be cost-efficient to advertise the availability of express service more widely.

The report recommended that state personnel scheduling renewal appointments (a small proportion of the application traffic) "more actively schedule appointments at Express Renewal offices" and that the state not establish any more express offices without ensuring that they would be no more expensive than traditional offices.

The express offices served a significantly higher percentage of clients between January and July 1987. For that period, the Pinellas County express offices increased the ratio of applicants served in that county to 6.1 percent for 5.5 percent of the staff used, and the Broward County express office served 2.3 percent of the applicants for 2.2 percent of the staff allocation.

## New Jersey[32]

### DESCRIPTION

For decades, the director of the Division of Motor Vehicles (DMV) in New Jersey appointed private individuals to run all 54 decentralized state offices that issue driver's and vehicle license applications and renewals (but do not give examinations). These agents served an indefinite term, but they could be removed with or without cause after 30 days' notice. They were often replaced after their political party was defeated. This system came under a great deal of public criticism.

The state provided offices for the agents in retail stores or elsewhere, including rent and utilities. As agents resign, they are being replaced by state employees.

All agencies are monitored and audited regularly (audits are quarterly), whether privately or state-run. The state has a special undercover investigative unit to handle major problems at the offices.

### ASSESSMENT

Client dissatisfaction with the service given by the private agents, which sometimes involved a wait as long as two hours for a driver's license, led to unfavorable media publicity. The DMV changed its policy in two ways, first, by replacing agents and their employees with state employees, with the goal of using state employees for all operations. Second, in March 1987, the DMV radically revised its contracts with the remaining private agents to require: a minimum number of hours the agency is open to the public, minimum wages set by the state for various grades of agency personnel, health insurance for all private employees (although not all fringe benefits accorded state workers), and a minimum number of personnel at each office.[33] The state also raised fees paid to private agents when they were not being paid enough to ensure an efficient operation.

Because these changes add to costs, cost comparisons done several years ago showing that agents saved the state money no longer apply. Agents are being phased out completely, so no cost comparisons are planned.

### Minnesota[34]

#### DESCRIPTION

For many years, Minnesota has had a system whereby driver's license applications are taken at the *county* level, either by county court clerks or by private individuals appointed by them to act as their agents. Motor vehicle license applications are taken at county auditor offices or by private individuals appointed by them to act as deputy registrars. The appointments of both agents and registrars are considered political.

Although the private citizens serving as deputies and agents are appointed by county officials, they are ultimately responsible to the state, which in fact issues the licenses. Private citizens appointed by county auditors and acting as deputy registrars issuing motor vehicle license applications may be removed by the state for poor performance, such as delay in sending in money collected from applicants. Private agents appointed by court clerks who are derelict in their duties are removed by the clerks.

The percentage of licenses issued by private agents and deputy registrars varies with the locality. Overall, about 90 percent of driver's license applications and renewals are taken by state employees at city halls, courthouses, and government multiservice centers and the remaining 10 percent by private agents. About half the motor vehicle license applications and renewals are taken at city halls, county courthouses, and multiservice centers and about half by deputy registrars (private individuals).

Private agents of county clerks (for driver's licenses) and deputy registrars (for motor vehicle licenses) are appointed for an indeterminate term, to be replaced only if their performance is judged unsatisfactory. County auditors write formal agreements with deputy registrars. They set up offices either in retail stores or malls, often as an adjunct to their own businesses. A private agent receives a 50-cent fee for each driver's license application or renewal. Deputy registrars receive $3.25 per application. Some have incorporated, and they can make $200,000–300,000 a year on motor vehicle license applications.

The main reasons for the counties' delegating work to private individuals were cost and convenience. The counties save money by not employing full-time state employees who receive fringe benefits for some of the licensing work. And citizens can apply for licenses after normal government business hours. Hennepin County, however, uses public employees at its multiservice centers and staggers their hours so that they are available as late as 8 or 9 p.m.

Twelve state field supervisors handle problems with the performance of agents or deputy registrars. They routinely visit each agent and deputy registrar two or three times a year.

State officials fill out an annual form for each deputy registrar. The form lists the number of errors in applications that were not caught by the deputy and compares the number with that for all other deputies. An office inventory and comments on the quality of the deputy registrar's staff are also included in the evaluation.

## ASSESSMENT

Problems with agents and registrars, mainly delays in sending fees to the state, are handled as they occur by the supervisors. In 1985–86, however, the state took eight months from the time it recognized a problem with a deputy registrar to his termination. During that time, the private registrar was $100,000 "behind" in his deposits. He began by being a day or two late, and the state was slow to recognize the extent of the problem.

The state has made no cost comparisons to determine whether using agents and deputies saves money. It seems on the surface that savings in rent and fringe benefits would be appreciable.

Because of occasional incidents of poor performance, some Minnesota legislators are critical of the system of deputizing, which inevitably becomes political when politicians are the ones who make the appointments. The state reports, however, that fewer than one deputy a year is "closed down."

### Summary of Findings and Recommendations on Driver's and Vehicle Licensing Services

A number of states have had substantial problems providing prompt, convenient driver's and motor vehicle license services to their citizens. States have been moving to open more offices in convenient locations and to permit more services by mail.

The experiment in Florida with license renewal offices in retail stores is intriguing. The concept of providing state services at convenient locations, in donated space, is an attractive one. The experiment appears to be working satisfactorily. Yet the number of outside offices, three, has not been increased since 1985, indicating that their use is limited. Expansion may be overly expensive. The reluctance to expand offices in donated retail space may also indicate that the initial problem of excessive waiting time at regular state offices has been alleviated.

Both Minnesota and New Jersey have used private individuals to process driver's and motor vehicle license applications for many years. Both states report difficulties, and New Jersey is converting to delivery by state employees. Their problems emphasize the need for performance standards agreements, careful monitoring of performance, and prompt action when problems come to light. Both states appear to have a political appointment process with an absence of normal competitive procurement practices. This practice does not seem to be good public policy.

Contracting, including a competitive bidding process, has not been tested in any of the states where officials were interviewed. Private organizations and public employees could compete to provide driver's and/or motor vehicle license services. Whether such operations could save money and, perhaps at the same time, provide more convenient services to the public is yet to be tested.

## TOLL BRIDGES AND TOLL ROADS OWNED AND/OR OPERATED BY THE PRIVATE SECTOR

Recent developments indicate possible new ways of supplying transportation infrastructure for states and local governments. Proposals both from private entrepreneurs and from governments to have private firms build and operate new bridges and roads that otherwise face major financial obstacles have become more common. Plans are being made for a toll bridge connecting cities in two states and for a toll road to be built by a private company and later turned over to the Commonwealth of Virginia. We know of no privately *owned* major roads or bridges in the United States.

### Toll Bridges[35]

The toll bridge discussed below involves two city governments rather than a state government, and it is in only the early planning stages. It is included here because of its potential interest to states.

The cities of Fargo, North Dakota and Moorhead, Minnesota, have signed a contract with the Municipal Development Corporation, a New York City-based for-profit firm, to build, own, and operate a toll bridge connecting the cities, to be completed in the spring of 1988. Approval of both states involved and the federal government was required.

A local construction firm, The Bridge Company, assembled an investment group to plan and propose the bridge. The company believes that this will be the first private toll bridge built in the United States in 40 years. Tax-exempt industrial development bonds for $1.6 billion were issued in December 1986 by the Municipal Development Corporation (MDC), based in New York City, to finance construction. MDC has the right to build and operate the bridge and collect tolls for 20 years after the bridge is complete. During that time, the company will be responsible for all repairs.

The agreement allows for two possible five-year renewals. Upon termination of the agreement, title to the bridge and the right to collect tolls go jointly to the two cities involved.

The agreement with the two cities allows the development company to set the tolls according to market conditions, with no government limits. Tolls may not be charged for pedestrians, bicycles, emergency vehicles, or passenger vehicles owned and operated by Moorhead or Fargo.[36] The contract for construction and operation of the bridge was not bid competitively, but it was negotiated with the engineering departments of the two cities.

The agreement requires that the bridge be maintained "in a state of good repair" in accordance with North Dakota and Minnesota highway department standards.[37] If the bridge is damaged or destroyed so that it is unusable, it must be replaced within one year.[38] The bridge becomes the property of the cities after 25 years unless the cities want to take possession five years later.[39] The cities may not construct a competing bridge during the first 20 years of the agreement unless they reimburse the franchisee for 90 percent of lost revenues resulting from construction of the new bridge.[40]

### Toll Roads

In April 1988, the governor of Virginia signed a bill enabling companies to build private toll roads. The immediate purpose of the legislation was to allow a private company to extend one of the state toll highways an additional 17 miles in Northern Virginia. The bill strikes down a 30-year-old ban against private toll roads.[41]

The company building the road said that it is economically feasible largely because most or all of the land will be donated. About 20 landowners who own necessary rights-of-way will give the property to the toll road company.[42]

The state will decide on the design and alignment layout and regulate the amount of all tolls charged at proposed toll highways and roads. Communities directly affected by a new highway must approve both the route and the amount of the tolls. The state will have limited supervision over all proceedings related to the construction and operation of the highway, which will revert to the state 10 years after construction bonds floated by the private construction firm are paid off. The proposed highway extension will be developed jointly by the Municipal Development Corporation, the Parsons Brickerhoff engineering firm, and the Kiewit Eastern construction firm. The road is expected to cost about $125 million and to be finished by late 1991. It will connect Dulles International Airport with far suburbs of Washington, D.C.

---

## *SUMMARY COMMENT ON TRANSPORTATION OPPORTUNITIES FOR THE PRIVATE SECTOR*

There seems little doubt that contracting for the types of road maintenance and repair that the private sector does particularly well, at costs comparable to using public employees, could be expanded. The jury is still out on the issuance of driver's and motor vehicle licenses by private deputies, and the toll bridge experiment will surely be watched with interest by states and localities with deflated pocketbooks.

---

### Notes

1. For a description of typical transportation assistance projects, see Wisconsin Expenditure Commission, "Privatization in Wisconsin State and Local Governments," October 1986, pp. 10–11.

2. Cheryl O'Ronk, *A Look at Using Contractors and Government Employees on Public Work Projects* (Lansing: Michigan Road Builders Association, Inc., 1986), p. 4.

3. This section is based on a telephone interview with Chuck Chitty, Chief, California Office of Highway Maintenance, October 1987, and materials received from him.

4. This section is based on a telephone interview with Joe Hill, Highway Liaison Engineer, Illinois Department of Transportation, November 1987, and materials received from him.

5. Ron Hagen, Office Administrator, Office for Maintenance, Iowa Department of Transportation, telephone interview November 1987, and materials received from him.

6. Ibid.

7. Bernhard H. Ortgies, Iowa Department of Transportation, "Iowa's Experience with General Contract Maintenance" [1984].

8. Adrian Clary, Engineer of Maintenance, Transportation Research Board, telephone interview, December 1987.

9. Ibid.

10. Ibid.

11. Ibid.

12. Ibid.

13. Ibid.

14. Don Casner, Acting Chief, Maintenance Division, Pennsylvania Department of Transportation, telephone interview, November 1987, and materials received from him.

15. Ibid.

16. Pennsylvania Service Purchase Contract, Pennsylvania Department of Transportation Maintenance District 1–4, with Pennsylvania Industries for the Blind and Handicapped, 15 April 1987.

17. Roy Jorgensen Associates, Inc., "Report to Pennsylvania Department of Transportation on Demonstration Area Contract Maintenance," 19 August 1981.

18. Ibid., pp. 4–21 and 4–22.

19. Ibid., p. 4–28.

20. Ibid., pp. 4–28 and 4–29.

21. Ibid., p. 4–31.

22. Ibid., pp. 5–1 to 5–4.

23. This section is based on telephone interviews with Stan Ather, Street Maintenance Engineer, and Wally Cohen, Purchasing, for the District of Columbia, December 1987.

24. This section is based on information from the Province of British Columbia, especially its newsletter "INFO LINE: Government Restructuring," editions of March 30, August 17, and September 6, 1988.

25. "A Look at Using Contractors and Government Employees on Public Work Projects," p. 73–80.

26. See "Iowa's Experience," table 2.

27. Ibid.

28. "A Look at Using Contractors and Government Employees on Public Work Projects."

29. This section is based on a telephone interview with R. J. Thompson, Driver's License Specialist, Florida Division of Drivers Licenses, November 1987, and materials received from him.

30. Ibid.

31. Florida Office of Management and Planning Services, "Evaluation of Driver License Express Renewal Offices One year after Inception," n.d. The remainder of this section is based on this report and a supplemental report on the workload in express offices as of September 1987.

32. This section is based on a telephone interview with Judy Kirkpatrick, Assistant Chief, Bureau of Agencies, New Jersey Division of Motor Vehicles, November 1987, and materials received from her.

33. New Jersey Division of Motor Vehicles, "Code of Conduct: Motor Vehicle Agents and Their Employees," 24 March 1987.

34. This section is based on telephone interviews with Marlene Swanson, Director, Division of Driver and Vehicle Services, Minnesota Department of Public Safety, November 1987 and materials received from Jane Brust, Deputy and Inspections Supervisor, Driver and Vehicle Services Division, Department of Public Safety.

35. This section is based on "Private Firms Will Build and Run a Toll Bridge," *Privatization*, 21 October 1987, p. 1, and telephone interviews with Bob Erickson, City Manager, Moorhead, Minnesota, and Nicholas Carlozzi, Chief Financial Officer, Municipal Development Corporation, with headquarters in New York City, November 1987, and materials received from them.

36. "Agreement between City of Fargo, North Dakota, and City of Moorhead, Minnesota, and Bridge Company," n.d., p. 6.

37. Ibid.

38. Ibid., p. 7.

39. Ibid., p. 8.

40. Ibid., p. 9.

41. "State Allows Private Toll Highways," *Privatization*, 7 May 1988, p. 3–4.

42. John Lancaster, "Private Operation of Dulles Toll Road Spur Is Backed," *Washington Post*, 10 February 1988, p. C4.

# Chapter Eight

# OVERALL FINDINGS AND RECOMMENDATIONS

*Harry P. Hatry*

The main intent of this volume is to provide states with examples of state experiments in making greater use of the private sector to deliver services. We have attempted to assess these experiments, based on the limited information available in terms of the experiments' success and problems that occurred and how they may have been corrected. The chapter endnotes indicate the state offices to be contacted for more information about specific efforts.

Here, we provide some overall findings and recommendations regarding private sector arrangements.

1. Use of the private sector to help deliver state services is not new, but it appears to be growing at an evolutionary—not revolutionary—rate.
2. Situational factors are important in determining the sources of new service delivery approaches. We cannot generalize as to the likely success of particular approaches for particular services. Nor, based on the cases reported here, can a universal statement be made that "approach X will always, or nearly always, bring improvements in delivery of service Y."

   Critical situational factors include:

   □ the level of efficiency and effectiveness of service delivery prior to changing approaches. If either was poor, a change has a much better chance of effecting improvements.
   □ the availability and quality of private suppliers. An example is the lack of bidders for special needs adoption services in the Louisville, Kentucky, area. The state has had to provide these services despite its preference for contracting. But agencies can attempt to influence provider availability. For example, as noted in chapter 7, when few providers bid on road maintenance and repair projects in Pennsylvania, regional managers contacted nonbidders to determine whether their

lack of participation was due to factors the state could change (e.g., the bidding process or the description of the work) so that requests for proposals (RFPs) could be made to attract more bidders. When Tennessee did not have enough bidders to operate a mental health facility, it identified two contract requirements as the likely cause (all state employees had to be retained at their existing compensation levels for nine months, and the contract had to be rebid after one year, with no automatic renewals). Similarly, New Hampshire was unable to contract for a mental health complex because all contractor personnel would report to a state employee. The point here is that state agencies having difficulty finding bidders may be able to make adjustments to increase the number of possible service providers.

□ how well the change is implemented. This factor includes the quality of the personnel that actually deliver the service and the quality of state's administration and monitoring (whether the service is contractual, involves volunteers or public-private partnerships, or is by some other arrangement). For example, two unsuccessful programs (South Carolina parks and recreation concessions and New Jersey motor vehicle and driver's license applications) were terminated because of dissatisfaction with contractor performance. Similarly, when New Mexico had two unsatisfactory experiences with contracting for prison food services, the availability of potential contractors enabled it to change providers three times in three years, ending in a satisfactory arrangement.

3. Key reasons for contracting include: (a) government difficulties in attracting qualified employees for some government activities and under existing working conditions (e.g., correctional food services and nurses for health care facilities), and (b) the desire to meet changing needs (e.g., corrections vocational programs) and new technology (e.g., medical services).

4. Most agencies that tested the use of private sector assistance did not have adequate evidence on how costs or quality changed after they implemented the new approach. Thus, neither the state agency nor others can usually pre-determine the effects of a new approach. State agencies considering the use of new service delivery approaches should identify the costs and quality of existing programs. When a change is subsequently made, the agency should track the costs and quality of the new delivery. These data enable the agency to make better decisions in the

future, to determine whether the change has succeeded, and if necessary, to consider further changes.

5. Implementation and management of these privatization arrangements clearly involve more than just securing a provider. A critical step involves fully specifying the provider's responsibilities in RFPs and contracts. Recommendations for developing contracts are presented in chapters 2, 3, 5, and 6. A classic example is that of New Mexico, which found it necessary to rewrite its RFP for prison food services three times, each becoming progressively more specific (e.g., specifying the amount of protein to be served daily) as a result of its dissatisfaction with contractors. Similarly, Kentucky had problems because its initial contract for operation of a correction facility did not explicitly identify responsibility for providing certain activities (e.g., providing a law library for inmates). When contracting with the private sector, agencies experienced problems with the contracting process and contract administration and monitoring process. These experiences indicate that agencies planning to contract should consider such actions as the following:

   □ RFPs and contracts should be explicit about important responsibilities, especially who does what and who pays for what. (Note: This recommendation is not intended to suggest that RFPs and contracts should specify in detail *how* the contractor is to do the job.)

   □ The agency should identify specific performance, such as service quality and quantity requirements, in the RFP and contracts.

   □ Agencies should monitor the performance of contractors and take corrective actions when performance is not what was expected by the agency or required by the contract.

6. As indicated above, a major aspect of managing agreements with the private sector is monitoring providers' performance. Some of the programs reviewed had significant problems because of insufficient monitoring. An extreme example is the corrections food services contract in Oklahoma. Inmates at an institution burned the facility down to protest meal quality. (Though food was not the whole story, it seems reasonable to assume that better monitoring could have helped prevent this disaster.) Monitoring is discussed in more detail in chapters 2, 3, 5, and 6. Monitoring is a concern not only with contracting but with other arrangements as well. Park officials, for example, emphasized the importance of tracking the performance of volunteers

to ensure satisfactory attendance and service quality. Indeed, monitoring service is appropriate to all service delivery alternatives, including delivery by state employees.

Monitoring can be handled in several ways. User feedback is an important but often unused method. New Mexico required its food service providers to distribute questionnaires on food service quality to inmates every three months. Florida conducted mail surveys of clients who used its contractor-provided license renewal offices. In addition, on-site inspections, both regularly scheduled and unannounced, are useful for evaluating the operation of facilities (whether the facilities are contracted, concessions, or operated by a private organization as part of a public-private partnership). Furthermore, providers in most instances should be required to submit detailed performance reports regularly. All agreements between the public and private parties should stipulate the kinds of monitoring and performance indicators to be used. Subsequently, performance monitoring should be a standard procedure.

7. Volunteers and public-private partnerships appear attractive, albeit limited, options. Volunteers were not used to a major extent by the agencies examined; they were used mainly for park operations and maintenance. Public-private partnerships were much more common, especially in parks and employment and training programs. For the partnerships, clear-cut guidelines on the responsibilities of the private partner are needed to protect the public interest.

8. A major problem with the use of volunteers is the lack of preparation of state supervisors, to increase their level of enthusiasm and ability to use volunteers effectively. In general, state agency programs using volunteers appear to have been too informal and did not provide explicit training to either the volunteers or their supervisors. Agencies did not provide specific guidelines on what to expect of volunteers or on how to monitor their performance and correct problems. Such guidelines and training of supervisors would strengthen volunteer programs. Chapter 3 provides more discussion of such needs.

9. Voucher systems (discussed in chapters 4 and 5) are an alternative to contracting and public employee delivery for some services, for example, day care and training programs. The use of vouchers widens the choice of suppliers available to clients, thus providing more convenient services. But it does not generally reduce costs significantly. The conditions under which

voucher systems seem most appropriate are identified in chapter 4 on Human Services.

10. By and large, major resistance from employees or their associations (e.g., unions) did not occur in the cases examined. These experiments, by and large, did not displace many public employees; in fact, use of volunteers, public-private partnerships, and vouchers seldom involve such displacements. Of the alternatives we examined, contracting is the one most likely to involve displacements. In many contracting cases we examined, contracting involved a new service or one that was being expanded. Kentucky's contract with a private firm for a new 200-bed minimum security correctional facility is an example.

    Yet employee resistance is natural. It should be expected when a significant number of displacements, especially layoffs, would occur. Then the agency needs to take steps to minimize the negative effects. The agency should reduce the work force through attrition, help displaced employees find other state jobs, provide training for available jobs, require contractors to give laid-off public employees first preference, and provide placement assistance. The estimated costs of these activities should be a part of the cost comparisons used when the states are considering a switch to contracting.

11. Given the fact that situational factors have a major effect on the success of a privatization arrangement (see number 2 above), pilot programs are sometimes useful. An example is the Iowa Department of Transportation experiment with contracts covering all road maintenance services. The pilot project encompassed four geographical areas. From it, the department concluded that this type of contract was not cost-effective but that contractors should be used for specific types of maintenance (chapter 7). Similarly, by contracting for a pilot project involving vouchers for day care, Pennsylvania administrators discovered major problems and recommended program changes leading to more efficient operation (chapter 4).

12. Whether or not pilot programs are undertaken, state agencies should perform a careful preanalysis before entering any arrangement involving a major change in how service is delivered. This type of analysis is beyond the scope of the present study, but other reports provide suggestions.[1]

Despite the many concerns, problems, and limitations noted above, many of these experiments with the greater use of the public sector appear reasonably successful. Periodic consideration by state agencies of alternative service delivery approaches is needed. When alternative approaches are being used—contracting, vouchers, volunteers, and public-private partnerships—agencies should review them periodically to determine whether a different approach, including service delivery by state personnel, is preferable.

---

**Note**

1. Among them are several reports by The Urban Institute and The Council of State Governments: "Building Innovation into Program Reviews: Analysis of Service Delivery Alternatives"; The Urban Institute Press, 1989; "State of Maryland Recommended Program Review Process," Maryland Department of Budget and Fiscal Planning, March 1987; and "State of Delaware Recommended Process for Analysis of Service Delivery Alternatives," Delaware Office of State Planning and Coordination, July 1987.

# SELECTED ANNOTATED BIBLIOGRAPHY

Behn, Robert D. "Managing Innovation in Welfare, Training, and Work: Some Lessons from ET Choices in Massachusetts." Paper presented at the annual meeting of the American Political Science Association, Chicago, 4 September 1987.

An objective analysis of the ET program in Massachusetts with some useful insights about its developing history and the strengths and weaknesses of its administration and achievements.

Camp, Camille K., and George M. Camp. "Private Sector Involvement in Prison Services and Operations." Prepared for the National Institute of Corrections, February 1984.

A comprehensive list and description, with some analysis, of the kinds of services provided by the private sector to local and state correctional facilities throughout the United States.

Chi, Keon S. *Alternative Service Delivery and Management Improvement in State Government.* Lexington, Ky.: Council of State Governments, 1987.

A fairly exhaustive bibliography of sources in the field of alternative service delivery and management productivity and improvement for state government. Includes sources on these subjects as applicable to local government.

———. "Privatization and Contracting for State Services: A Guide." *Innovations,* Council of State Governments, April 1988.

A concise but helpful summary of the extent of contracting in state government, of how to analyze whether to contract, and how to write contracts.

Connecticut Public/Private Partnership Commission. "Contracting-Out Selected Functions of the Connecticut Department of Motor Vehicles and Other State Agencies. Phase I: Preliminary Feasibility Study." 30 June 1986.

A discussion of some pros and cons of contracting in these areas.

Council of State Governments. *State and Local Government Purchasing,* 2d ed. Lexington, Ky.: Council of State Governments, 1983.

A lengthy survey of the details of government purchasing, both state and local: accountability, impartiality, competence, openness, and value.

Hackett, Judith, et al. *Issues in Contracting for the Private Operation of Prisons and Jails.* Washington, D.C.: National Institute of Justice, 1987. Although this report is focused on prisons, a discussion of most of the 23 issues analyzed is also appropriate to contracting for residential facilities in other service areas. Covers legal issues, policy and program issues, decisions to be made before deciding whether to contract, appropriate contents for requests for proposals and contracts, and needs for contract monitoring and evaluation of the contracting approach.

Hatry, Harry P., and Eugene Durman. *Issues in Competitive Contracting for Social Services.* Falls Church, Va.: The National Institute of Governmental Purchasing, Inc., 1985.
A discussion of a number of issues in contracting for various human services, with a special focus on encouraging constructive competition in these services.

Hatry, Harry P., et al. "Building Innovation into Program Reviews: Analysis of Service Delivery Alternatives." Washington, D.C.: Urban Institute Press. June 1989.
The lessons learned from the work of The Urban Institute in 1986 and 1987 with teams from several departments of state government in Maryland and Delaware.

Kettner, Peter M., and Lawrence L. Martin. *Purchase of Service Contracting.* Newbury Park, Mich.: Sage Publications, 1986.
A treatment of the basic elements of purchase of service contracts that are particularly applicable in the area of human services.

Massachusetts, State of, Office of Human Resources. "Final Report of the Governor's Day Care Partnership Initiative." June 1987.
A detailed discussion of the Massachusetts initiative.

Michigan Road Builders Association, Inc. *A Look to Using Contractors and Public Employees on Public Work Projects.* Lansing: Michigan Road Builders Association, Inc., 1986.
Catalog by states of the kinds of construction and maintenance done by state employees and by contractors in each jurisdiction and the allocation of the work to each group.

New Jersey State and Local Expenditure and Revenue Policy Commission. "Alternative Methods for Delivering Public Services in New Jersey." February 1987.
A quite detailed discussion of the pros and cons of alternative service delivery in New Jersey.

Oregon, State of. "Guidelines for Contracting State Work," n.d.
A short but helpful report suggesting guidelines for state agencies considering contracting state work: general advice for making contracting decisions. Includes a model cost comparison for using state workers and "Contractor A" and "Contractor B" for custodial services for a state college.

Pennsylvania Legislative Budget and Finance Committee. "Report on a Per-

formance Audit of the Administration of Pennsylvania's Subsidized Child Day Care System," September 1987.
A substantive report on the subsidized day care system in Pennsylvania.

Roy Jorgensen Associates, Inc. "Report to Pennsylvania Department of Transportation on Demonstration Area Contract Maintenance," 19 August 1981.
Report on the Pennsylvania 18-month experiment whereby contractors were made responsible for certain segments of roadway for *all* maintenance on those segments instead of contracting for specific aspects of road maintenance.

Savas, E. S. *Privatization: The Key to Better Government*. Chatham, N.J.: Chatham House, 1987.
Discusses in detail the concepts involved for many of the ways to make greater use of the private sector and presents many examples from many public services—primarily from an advocate's perspective.

Short, John. *The Contract Cookbook for Purchase of Services*. Lexington, Ky.: Council of State Governments, 1987.
The details of decision making and contract writing in the field of contracting for government service. Written for the National Association of State Purchasing Officials and the Council of State Governments.

University of Texas at Austin, Lyndon B. Johnson School of Public Affairs. "Contracting Selected State Government Functions: Issues and Next Steps," 1986.
Detailed coverage of the issues of contracting for various state department functions in Texas.

———. "Contracting Selected State Government Functions: Legislation and Implementation," 1987.
The details of legalizing various new areas of state contracting and implementing such contracting.

Virginia Department of Planning and Budget. "The Feasibility of Contracting in Virginia's Mental Health and Mental Retardation Facilities." 1987.
The pros and cons of contracting in these areas of human services.

Washington Legislative Budget Committee. "Performance Audit: Prison Education and Training Programs." 19 August 1977.
An interesting assessment of the delivery of education programs in the State of Washington and the pros and cons of contracting some of that delivery.

Washington Department of Corrections. "Report to the Legislature: Academic and Vocational Training." 12 October 1981.
A follow-up report to the report above assesses the quality of academic and vocational training in the Washington Department of Corrections.

Wisconsin Expenditure Commission. "Final Report [Privatization]." December 1986.

A thoughtful report on various kinds of contracting for state services in Wisconsin.

————. "Final Report Summary [Privatization]." December 1986.

An executive summary of the above report.

————. "Privatization in Wisconsin State and Local Governments." October 1986.

An earlier assessment of contracting in state and local government in Wisconsin.

JOAN W. ALLEN was a major contributor to an exploratory analysis of prison privatization "Contracting in the Private Sector for the Operation of State Correctional Facilities" published by the National Institute of Justice in 1987. She also participated recently in research for "The Capital Investment and Maintenance Decision Process in the Public Sector," a report for the National Council on Public Works Improvement.

KEON S. CHI is a senior policy analyst at The Council of State Governments and teaches political science at Georgetown College. His area of specialization is state policy innovations. He is the author of numerous articles, books, chapters and monographs on public policy and management issues including "Privatization and Contracting for State Services: A Guide."

KEVIN M. DEVLIN is a Research Assistant in the Center for Management and Administration at the Council of State Governments. He has authored papers on a variety of subjects, including "Drug Testing for State Employees, Federal Reimbursement Regulations, and Serving the Mentally Ill Offender: Hawaii's Approach and Other State Efforts."

MARK FALL is a Research Associate at The Urban Institute. His research work has been on a variety of topics of importance to state and local government, including economic development, education, performance measurement, and privatization. He received a bachelors degree from the University of California, Los Angeles and a master's degree in Public Administration, with concentration in Intergovernmental Management, from the University of Southern California.

HARRY P. HATRY is a Principal Research Associate and Director of the State and Local Government Research Program at The Urban Institute. He is a member of the National Academy of Public Administration and is on the Editorial Board of "New Directions for Program Evaluation, Evaluation Review, National Civic Review, and The Bureaucrat." He has written widely on program evaluation and related topics, and received the 1984 American Society for Public Administration Management Science Section award as the "Outstanding Contributor to the Literature of Management Science and Policy Science."

*WAYNE MASTERMAN* was a research associate at the Center for Management and Administration at the Council of State Governments. He participated in privatization feasibility studies in Delaware, Maryland and Virginia. Currently he is the editor of the *Kentucky Coal Journal.*